Country Gifts

Handmade & Homebaked

by Eileen Westfall

Country Gifts

Handmade & Homebaked

by Eileen Westfall

Meredith® Press
New York

Meredith® Press is an imprint of Meredith® Books
President, Book Group: Joseph J. Ward
Vice-President, Editorial Director: Elizabeth P. Rice

For Meredith® Press
Executive Editor: Maryanne Bannon
Associate Editors: Carolyn Mitchell, Ruth Weadock
Copy Editor: Candie Frankel
Production Manager: Bill Rose
Book Designer: Diane Wagner
Cover photograph, Robert Gattullo; styling, Diane Wagner.
Photography by Shel Izen.
Graphic arts by Nancy Rowland of Sound Images, Inc.
Piping art on pages 20–21 by Darrel Young.

ISBN: 0-696-04666-0
Library of Congress Catalog Card Number: 93-077577

Printed in the United States of America.
10 9 8 7 6 5 4 3 2 1

Acknowledgments

Thanks to the many people who assisted in the preparation of this book:

Sherry and Bob Budke, Linda Currie, Alma Galgiani, Lisel Greenfield, Daniel Kurth, Lila Kurth, Robin Page, and Karen Perkins, for testing the recipes and cooking the food samples;

Linda Cook, Linda Currie, Sally Covert Evans, Esther Hoth, Shel Izen, Susie Kirk, Daniel Kurth, Rita McIntosh, Dorothy Powell, Sandi Smith-Grove, and Evie Wiviott, for sharing their family recipes;

Robin Page and Alma Galgiani, for creating original recipes;

Julie Anderson, James Bishop-Elliot, and Rhonda Kray, for the generous loan of their china for photography;

Monica M. Hahn, for the tatted snowflakes;

The ladies of Silkworm Designs in Benecia, California, for use of their props;

All the nice people at Action Photo Lab;

Darrel Young, for the piping illustrations;

And my agent, Elizabeth Pelham.

To my grandmother
Inga Haugen Kurth
who created many handmade country gifts

Dear Crafter,

As the seasons pass and we celebrate the holidays and special occasions of each year, so many opportunities arise to make or bake something special for friends and family. Now you can bring the creative spirit of crafting and baking to the joyful spirit of giving.

In *Country Gifts Handmade & Homebaked*, you'll find delightful projects for gift-giving—from natural wreaths and functional baskets to tiny country quilts and pretty pillows. Add an extra sweet touch by incorporating a batch of delicious homebaked cookies, a tin of aromatic tea mix, or a plate of sumptuous mini cheesecakes, all made with love by you. Recipients are sure to appreciate your efforts, as each gift you give shines with your own special touch.

All of the projects and recipes are depicted in beautiful color photographs, accompanied by complete, step-by-step instructions and helpful illustrations. A handy "basics" chapter offers tips and techniques for everything from quilting to candy-making. Many of these gifts can be completed in a weekend, so you'll always have a source on hand for last-minute surprises and early newborns!

We hope you enjoy *Country Gifts* for many seasons of birthdays, holidays, special days and joyous occasions to come.

Sincerely,

Maryanne Bannon

Maryanne Bannon, Executive Editor

Table of Contents

Introduction

As long as I can remember, I have valued handmade things. My grandmother was a quilter, and she also loved to embroider and crochet. She lived a long distance from me, but I looked forward to our family visits because her house was always packed with quilts, pillows, and stitchery of all kinds.

I am lucky to have been presented with many unique handmade items since early childhood. The first gift I ever received was a handmade doll that my aunt sent me the day I was born. The doll was sewn from green mattress ticking, and she had wool yarn for hair and an embroidered face. Her name was Gretel and I loved her dearly. Another memory I treasure is of a maroon sweater my mom knit for me when I was in the first grade. It had a cable-stitch pattern, and embroidered multicolor flowers danced up and down the front. I thought it was the most beautiful sweater in the world, and I was so proud the first day I wore it to school! Over the years, many more treasures came my way. My grandma sent me quilts and embroidered pillowcases. What a thrill it was to open the packages and find something Grandma had made with her own hands.

Just as I received handmade gifts when I was young, today I find myself keeping the tradition alive. When there are celebrations for any of my friends or family, I usually design and make a gift myself. It is my way of saying, "You are a one-of-a-kind, treasured person to me." I just finished a baby quilt (using the miniature star pattern found on page 102) for the first baby of my husband's cousin. I thought of the new parents-to-be every day as I stitched the blocks together and waited anxiously for news of the baby's arrival. I raced along with my quilting, hoping I would finish in time! The

baby came just as I sewed the last few stitches, and the thank-you note I received said they would treasure the quilt forever as a family heirloom!

You, too, probably have memories of special gifts made for you long ago or perhaps recently. Remember how good it feels to know someone took the time and care to make something just for you? *Country Gifts—Handmade & Homebaked* is a collection of projects and directions for those times when you want to make unique gifts for those dear to you. Suitable for year-round giving, they include gifts for each of the four seasons, for special occasions, such as birthdays and anniversaries, and for holidays. Each project includes a recipe, so that you can make not only the gift container but also a special treat to accompany it. I always tuck in a copy of the recipe so that the person receiving the gift can prepare and serve the dish at another time.

In a time when commercially marketed gifts tend to look alike and often lack inspiration, it is a pleasure indeed to be able to create gifts that you know will be enjoyed, appreciated, remembered—and enjoyed again.

I am sure your family and friends will take great pleasure in receiving your original handmade gifts. And though I am confident you will find great joy in creating for others, please don't be shy about making some of these projects for your own home as well!

Warmly,

Eileen Westfall

Eileen Westfall

Getting Started
Tips and Techniques

❧

*Whether you're a seasoned crafter or just starting out, you'll find a wealth
of helpful hints and reminders here, to ensure successful stitching and
the best baking for all your country gifts.*

Sewing Basics

Having the right tools and knowing how to use them can make a noticeable difference in the quality of your finished projects. This section provides information on tools and fabric selection that will make your sewing easier and more pleasurable.

Equipment

For optimum results, use good-quality equipment. In addition to a sewing machine, hand and machine needles, pins, and thread, you will need tools for cutting and marking fabric. My favorites are described below. I think that once you start using them, you will find them indispensable!

GLUE STICKS

Use glue sticks to hold fabric shapes in place for appliqué. Because they have a waxy base, glue sticks are neat, clean, and easy to use. Be sure the brand you choose is suitable for fabric.

LIGHT BOXES

A tabletop light box is a handy piece of equipment for marking patterns, templates, quilting designs, embroidery designs, and other shapes on fabric. Available in many sizes, a light box is a low, rectangular frame with a smooth, translucent drawing surface that is illuminated from behind with one or more bulbs or tubes. When you place the pattern and the fabric to be marked on top of it, the pattern lines can be seen through the fabric and readily transferred.

MARKING PENS

Erasable marking pens are available with two different kinds of ink: fading and wash-out. Fading inks make light marks that disappear with time upon exposure to air. One disadvantage is that the marks may fade before a project is completed. To avoid having to re-mark a project, I use fading ink markers only on small projects that I know I will be completing quickly. Wash-out inks generally leave brighter, darker markings. These marks disappear when the fabric is wet but unfortunately can reappear when the fabric dries. The fabric may have to be rewet many times before the markings disappear completely.

QUILTING TAPE

For more professional quilting, try using quilting tape. Quilting tape is a narrow (¼") paper masking tape available in hardware stores and quilt supply shops. The tape is applied directly onto the item being quilted and serves as a guide for the quilter to follow, resulting in a line of quilting stitches that is perfectly straight. Quilting tape is relatively inflexible, so it is not suitable for marking curves.

ROTARY CUTTER

Rotary cutters and thick acrylic see-through rulers have revolutionized patchwork. I highly recommend them, for they enable you to make precision straight cuts in a fraction of the time it takes to cut with scissors. If you have never used a rotary cutter before, stop into your fabric or quilt shop and ask about classes in learning how to use one properly. Practice your rotary cutting skills using scrap fabric and develop your proficiency before cutting into good fabric. Without the proper preparation, you could cut yourself or ruin your fabric.

Always work on a self-healing mat when using a rotary cutter to protect your work surface and prolong the life of the round cutting blade. Self-healing mats are made of a resilient plastic. Even the deepest cuts appear to heal themselves, leaving only light scratch marks visible on the surface. Most cutting mats have ruler markings along the outer edges and a grid in the center for easy measuring and accurate cutting.

SCISSORS

Reserve one pair of scissors for cutting fabric only, and keep several others on hand for cutting paper and other materials. For smooth, accurate cutting, keep all of your scissors in good condition and sharpen them when they become dull.

SEAM RIPPER

When you sew a project that includes exacting patchwork, mistakes are bound to happen. If you make a mistake, don't try picking out the bad stitches with a pin—it will take forever and you will get discouraged. Use a seam ripper instead, to cut through the stitches quickly. Pick out the loose threads before you restitch the seam. As long as you correct the error neatly, no lasting harm will be done.

Fabric

Many crafters pride themselves on amassing great quantities of fabric just so they will have the right color or print on hand for new projects—and then they go out and buy new fabric when inspiration strikes! I wonder how many thousands of yards of fabric lie quietly in closets all over the world waiting to be used! Whatever your philosophy of fabric buying may be, here are a few tips you may find helpful as you plan for the projects in this book.

CHOOSING COLORS

Color is as important as design in determining whether or not your projects are aesthetically pleasing. When you are making gifts for friends, be sure to consider their color tastes and decorating schemes. It would be a shame to work hard on a housewarming gift, only to discover your friends have it stored away because it doesn't coordinate with the colors or look of their new home. Pay attention to seasonal colors too. Pink, yellow, and blue are perfect for Easter gifts but wouldn't make sense for a Halloween treat bag.

The Color Wheel. To choose colors for your projects, it helps to know a bit about the colors that appear on the color wheel and how they relate to one another. The three primary colors—the colors from which all other colors are derived—are yellow, red, and blue. The secondary colors are orange, violet, and green. The tertiary colors are yellow-orange, red-orange, red-violet, blue-violet, blue-green, and yellow-green. White, black, gray, and beige are neutral tones; they are not considered colors and do not appear on the color wheel. A tint is created when white is added to a color. A shade is created when black is added to a color.

Color Schemes. There are three main types of color schemes: monochromatic, analogous, and complementary. A monochromatic scheme combines shades or tints of the same color, such as pink, rose, and burgundy. An analogous scheme combines related colors, or those that are next to each other on the color wheel, such as yellow, yellow-green, and green. A complementary scheme combines colors that are opposite each other on the wheel, such as red and green.

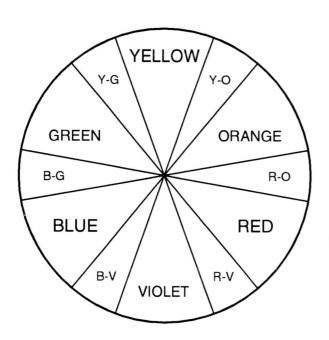

COLLECTING SCRAPS

Almost all the projects featured in this book can be sewn using very little fabric. I store fabric scraps for small projects in zip-lock plastic bags according to color. I put as many pieces of one color family in each bag as I can. That way, when I am looking for a particular color for a project, I can quickly get a general idea of how much fabric I have on hand. I enjoy saving scraps of truly wonderful fabric, and I find it a challenge to use them successfully in meaningful projects.

FABRIC CONTENT

If you save odd pieces of fabric or have collected fabric over the years, you may no longer know what the fiber content is. You should use only 100 percent cotton fabric for the projects in this book. Polyester fabrics and blends pucker and pull, whereas all-cotton fabrics have more give so that patchwork seams can be pressed smooth and flat. If you are uncertain of the fiber content, test the fabric for clues.

The Flame Test. Pull a few threads from the fabric, and carefully hold them over a flame. Burning polyester and other synthetics give off black smoke and smell faintly of plastic.

The Iron Test. Iron a crease into the fabric, then examine it. The creases in all-cotton fabrics appear sharper and crisper than those in polyester or other synthetics.

Making the Projects

Each project in this book includes a list of supplies, a cutting guide for the fabric pieces, and directions with patterns and diagrams. Before you attempt a project, read through the tips and suggestions in this section. It includes detailed information on patterns, sewing, quilting, embroidery, appliqué, and finishes. If you are a beginner, use this section as a guide to the basics when you are ready to work these details. If you are more experienced, you will find this section a valuable "refresher course."

Patterns and Templates

The project patterns, embroidery designs, and quilting motifs are printed actual-size whenever possible. Actual-size templates are provided for all patchwork shapes. All patterns and templates include a ¼" seam allowance.

Using a Half-Pattern. Some large patterns and embroidery motifs are printed as half-patterns. The center of each motif is clearly labeled. To make a full pattern, trace the half-pattern twice on separate sheets of tracing paper. Turn one tracing wrong side up and place it alongside the other tracing, matching the center markings. When the two tracings are aligned, tape the two halves together to form the complete pattern. Some half-patterns can be used as is. Place the indicated edge on the fabric fold and cut through both thicknesses. Unfold the fabric for a full-size piece.

Cutting Strips. Additional strips, squares, and rectangles needed to make a project are listed under the cutting guide, along with any pieces to be cut from patterns or templates. The cutting guide

specifies the fabric from which to cut the piece and the length and width. The ¼" seam allowance is included in the dimensions. Use a rotary cutter and thick acrylic see-through ruler to measure and cut these shapes quickly and accurately.

Preparing the Fabric

The yardages listed under each project's supplies assume a 45" fabric width. If the fabric you use is not 45" wide, you may have to adjust the amount shown. Most projects use so little fabric, a variance in width will not affect the amount needed. Exceptions are the Sailboat Tote (page 40) and the Evergreen Tote (page 169). Specific dimensions for the backing, filling, and other project pieces are listed in the cutting guides. These amounts are more specific than the yardages and amounts listed with the supplies.

Before you cut into the fabric, preshrink it by washing and drying it just as you would the finished item. To remind myself which of my fabrics I have prewashed, I press a bright self-adhesive sticker onto one corner of each piece. When you are ready to begin a project, press the fabric you will be using with a hot steam iron. It is essential to eliminate all wrinkles and folds, which can prevent the cutout fabric shapes from being exact.

Marking the Fabric

Accurate cutting is the heart of successful sewing, especially when the pattern pieces are small. No amount of fussing in the later stages of a project can correct the errors that compound when inaccurate templates and patterns are introduced at the beginning. The fabric must be properly handled and marked before the first cut is even made.

Unless specifically directed to do otherwise, plan to cut all patterns, templates, and strips so that a straight edge runs along the lengthwise or crosswise grain of the fabric. Edges cut on the bias, or diagonal, of the fabric will have extra stretch and may not fit the edges of the other pieces smoothly and accurately.

If you don't have a light box for marking your fabric (page 12), make paper templates and patterns instead. Simply trace the template or pattern outline, then cut out the shape on the marked line. Turn the fabric right side up, lay the template or pattern on top, and trace around the edges with a fabric marking pen. I like to glue sandpaper to the back of my paper templates before I cut them out. The sandpaper adds weight and sturdiness to the paper, and the rough gritty surface helps to grip the fabric for a more accurate cut. Be sure to cut sandpaper only with old, dull shears, so that you won't ruin your good scissors.

If you would rather not use a marking pen, simply pin the paper pattern or template to the fabric for cutting. Space the pins close together and close to the pattern edges, to prevent the paper from wrinkling or bowing and thus distorting the piece as you cut.

One "marking" method I strongly discourage is the hold-and-cut technique. Sewing small pieces is an exact art, and holding a template against the fabric with one hand while cutting with the other can only lead to ill-shaped, ill-fitting fabric pieces and much frustration. You will be more satisfied with the finished results if you take a few moments' extra time to properly mark the fabric or pin a pattern to it. Cut out the pieces carefully, using a rotary cutter for straight edges and your best sewing shears for curves.

Sewing and Patchwork

Perfectly cut fabric shapes will not by themselves make a successful project—they must be sewn together with care and precision. The five steps that follow will ensure that your sewing proceeds smoothly, whether you are working on a small patchwork block with straight seams or a project with curved seams.

1. Pin or baste the fabric pieces together.
To prevent the fabric from slipping before or during stitching, pin or baste the seams to be joined. Basting is best done with a contrasting color thread, as it will be easier to see and remove later on.

2. Use short stitches.
Set the sewing machine for short straight stitches, about 12 per inch. Long loose stitches can come undone, but small stitches will add to the overall strength of the seam.

3. Back-tack the seams.
Stitch back and forth a short distance at both ends of a seam, to prevent it from coming undone.

4. Maintain uniform seam allowances.
Even a small variation from the specified ¼" seam allowance can cause the fabric pieces to be ill-fitting and the overall project to become distorted, especially when many small pieces are sewn together. If your sewing machine doesn't have a stitching guide, lay a piece of tape on the machine plate exactly ¼" from the needle to act as a guide.

5. Press the seam allowance toward the darker fabric.
After stitching individual pieces, strips, or blocks, press all seam allowances toward the darker fabrics. Pressing the seam allowance in this manner will prevent darker seam allowances from showing through lighter fabrics on the front of the project.

It will also reduce fabric bulk under the lighter-colored fabrics, making them easier to quilt and embroider.

Quilting

Quilting is a three-step process used to sew a fabric, batting, and usually a backing fabric together. First, the quilt layers are basted together, then the quilting stitches are sewn through all the layers, and finally, the basting stitches are removed, allowing the quilting design to pop out. On very small projects, basting may not be required.

All but two of the quilted projects in this book use outline quilting exclusively. Outline quilting stitches follow the contour of a seam or appliqué. Outline quilting is worked ¼" from the edge, and can appear on either the inside or the outside of the patchwork or appliqué shape. Sometimes outline quilting appears right next to the seam or appliqué, as in the Sprinkling Can Cover (page 29).

Motif quilting is a design worked independently of the patchwork or appliqué in a solid, open area. The Miniature Star Quilt (page 102) and the Sailboat Tote (page 40) feature motif quilting. The Miniature Star Quilt has quilted X's on its plain blocks, and the Sailboat Tote has parallel lines on some of the plain blocks. You will find details on how to mark and work these quilting motifs in the project directions.

Embroidery

Many of the embroidery designs in this book are featured on small pieces of fabric. For easier stitching, work the embroidery before cutting the pattern piece. Place the fabric in an embroidery hoop to hold it taut during stitching. Use two or three strands of embroidery floss in the needle for each of the four basic stitches described here.

BACKSTITCH

Bring the needle up through the fabric so the thread emerges on the right side (A). Insert the needle about ⅛" to the right (B) and guide the needle tip out about ⅛" to the left (C), so the original exit stitch A is in the center. Pull the thread snug. Continue stitching in a smooth, rhythmic motion, by inserting the needle ⅛" to the right and bringing it out ⅛" to the left of the previous exit stitch.

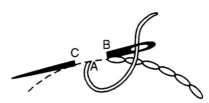

CHAIN STITCH

Bring the needle up through the fabric so the thread emerges on the right side (A). Insert the needle close to the same point (B). Guide the needle tip out ⅛"–³⁄₁₆" away (C), keeping the working thread under the needle tip. Pull the needle through and draw the loop snug. Repeat to form chain stitch.

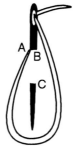

FRENCH KNOT

Bring the needle up through the fabric so the thread emerges on the right side (A). Wrap the thread around the needle two or three times. Insert the needle close to A. Use your free hand to pull the thread snug around the needle, then draw the needle through the fabric to the wrong side, making a tight knot.

SATIN STITCH

Bring the needle up through the fabric so the thread emerges at the topmost point of the area to be filled (A). Insert the needle into the fabric at the bottommost point of the area to be filled (B). Continue, bringing the new stitch out at the top (C) and reinserting it at the bottom (D) immediately to the right of the previous stitch. Fill right side of area first, then return to center top and fill left side in same manner.

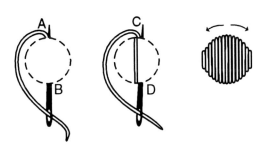

Appliqué

Appliqué is the technique of stitching one fabric shape onto another to form a decorative picture or design. Appliqué can be worked by hand (for a traditional look) or by sewing machine (for a modern look). All but two of the appliquéd projects in this book were stitched by hand, but you may sew any of them by hand or machine, as you choose. Basic directions follow and are easily adapted to the individual projects.

HAND APPLIQUÉ

Many different methods of hand appliqué have been devised, all with good-looking results. My preferred method uses a paper template, which I find makes the hand stitching a pleasure instead of a chore. Here's how to proceed:

1.   Cut out the fabric shape to be appliquéd (including seam allowance) using a paper pattern.

2.   Trim off the seam allowance from the paper pattern (or a copy of it, if you wish to reuse the pattern) to make a template.

3.   Place the fabric shape wrong side up on a flat surface and center the template on top. Fold the fabric seam allowance evenly over the edges of the template, and baste all around.

4.   Press the entire piece with a hot steam iron to flatten the seam allowance and crease the folded edge. Let cool a few moments, then remove the basting thread and paper template from the appliqué.

5.   Using a glue stick, affix the appliqué to the right side of the background fabric, being careful to position it in the exact spot desired. Press it with a warm iron to secure.

6. Sew the appliqué to the background fabric with tiny overcast stitches; insert the needle into the background fabric underneath the appliqué, instead of next to it, to hide the stitches.

MACHINE APPLIQUÉ

Machine appliqué uses a close zigzag stitch to secure the fabric appliqué to the background fabric. It is much faster to work than hand appliqué, though the edges can fray more readily than hand appliqué after repeated machine washing. Here's how to proceed:

1. Cut out the fabric shape to be appliquéd on the stitching line; do not include a seam allowance.

2. Using a glue stick, affix the appliqué to the right side of the background fabric, being careful to position it in the exact spot desired. Press it with a warm iron to secure.

3. Cut a piece of tear-away nonwoven interfacing slightly larger than the appliqué.

4. Slip the interfacing piece under the background fabric, so it is directly behind and extending slightly beyond the glued appliqué shape. Pin in place from the right side. (The interfacing will add stability to the fabrics during stitching.)

5. Set the sewing machine for close-set zigzag stitches about ⅟₁₆" wide (machine satin stitch). Test the flow of stitching and the tension of the machine on scrap fabric; if the stitches or fabric bunch up, loosen the tension or reset the machine for stitches spaced a little further apart.

6. Zigzag-stitch all around the edges of the appliqué. Be sure to cover the edges completely to prevent future fraying.

7. After you have completed the sewing, carefully tear away the interfacing from the wrong side of the backing fabric.

Bias Binding

Many of the projects in this book require bias binding to finish the edges—most often, you will be binding the edges of a "sandwich" made up of quilt top, batting, and backing. Because the binding is made from strips of fabric cut on the bias, or diagonal, of the fabric, it has the flexibility to turn corners and curves smoothly. You can use purchased bias binding, available by the package in sewing supply stores, or you can make your own binding. Purchased tape is more convenient to use. For an original designer look, you may prefer to make your own binding using fabric in the pattern and color of your choice.

TO MAKE BINDING

For a finished binding ⅝" wide, you must start with a bias strip 1¾" wide (see step 1). To make wider or narrower binding, adjust the starting width by ¼" for every ⅛" increment in the finished binding. Here's how to proceed:

1. Measure and cut a large square of fabric that includes two selvage edges. Mark a line across the fabric diagonally, from corner to corner. Mark several parallel lines on either side, spacing them 1¾" apart.

Cutting & Sewing Bias Binding

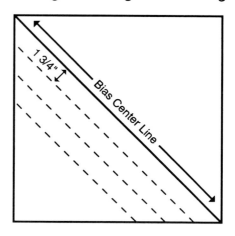

2. Using a rotary cutter, trim away the selvages of the fabric and cut the strips on the marked lines. (Save the corner triangular pieces for another project.)

3. Angle the strips. end to end and right sides facing, and stitch together.

Stitch strip ends together like this:

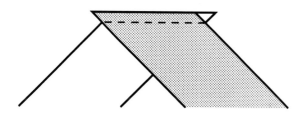

Not this:

4. Press the seams open. Trim off the excess seam allowance even with the binding edge.

TO APPLY BINDING

Purchased bindings and those you make yourself are applied the same way to finish raw fabric edges. If you are using purchased binding, just skip any folding and pressing steps described below that have been completed during the manufacturing. Here's how to proceed:

1. Cut a length of binding equal to the perimeter of the project piece plus 2½". (Trim the ends straight across, not on an angle.)

2. Press one short edge, then one long edge ¼" to the wrong side.

3. Beginning on a straight or curved edge (not in a corner), pin the binding all around the quilted piece, right sides facing and unpressed raw edges matching. Overlap the short ends ½", so the folded end is on the bottom, and trim off any excess. Baste in place.

4. Machine-stitch ¼" from the outer edge all around. Turn corners in the usual way: Stop with the needle down in the fabric, lift the presser foot, and rotate the entire piece 90 degrees. Move the excess binding out of the stitching path, then lower the presser foot and continue.

5. Remove the basting thread. Fold the binding to the wrong side of the piece, covering the raw edges. Pin so that the folded edge of the binding conceals the machine stitching, and whipstitch in place all around.

Piping

Piping consists of a cord encased in a fabric strip. The edges of the fabric are stitched together, providing a seam allowance that can be joined into a project's seams for a neat, tailored finish. Piping can be handmade, but I prefer using prepacked piping, which is available in a wide range of colors to coordinate with a variety of projects. Here's how to prepare piping that will be joined in a seam:

1. Cut a length of piping equal to the perimeter of the project piece plus 1". Using a seam ripper, pick out the stitches at each end for ¾".

2. Fold back the piping fabric and trim off ½" of cord.

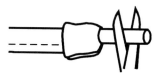

3. Turn the loose fabric end to the inside, even with the end of the cord.

4. Using a zipper foot, restitch along the previous stitching line.

5. Prepare the opposite end of the piping in the same way, so the ends butt smoothly.

6. Pin the piping all around the project piece, right sides facing and edges matching, so the finished ends butt together. Using a zipper foot, sew the piping ⅜6" from the edge all around. When you add the fabric backing, sew ¼" from the edge, for a snug piping join.

About the Recipes

Have you ever opened a cookbook and tried a great-sounding recipe only to have it turn out different from the picture or not at all? It's happened to me more than once. When I decided to write a book with both crafts and recipes, I wanted time-tested, reliable recipes that were real winners! I went to my friends and told them I was looking for favorite family recipes—foods so tasty and exceptional they could be given as gifts. All of my friends became interested in my quest and wanted to contribute. Through their generosity, you are receiving recipes that have been in some families for years and years. Some friends who are very creative, accomplished cooks decided to develop original recipes just for this book.

I have tasted each recipe myself, and I supervised the making of every sample photographed. Each one is perfect for gift-giving. To ensure that you have the best results, I have assembled some simple guidelines and tips to help you as you cook and bake.

Equipment

BAKING PANS

Always use the pan size specified in the recipe to ensure that baked goods rise to the proper height and have the right texture and moistness. When I was planning the baked samples for photography, I wrote down a larger pan size on one recipe by mistake. When my friend Karen returned with small, flat Pumpkin Squares, I knew something had gone wrong somewhere. As I looked over the recipe, I discovered that I had goofed on the pan size. I corrected my error, and the new batch came out perfectly.

CANDY THERMOMETER

I used to think that a candy thermometer would be too hard to use. I had attempted the hard ball/soft ball method of testing doneness without much success, and as a result, I felt more confused than ever about my candy-making ability. Then one day, a friend told me about a fudge recipe she had made using a candy thermometer. Her success story inspired me to buy one (I found one at a grocery store for under three dollars) and give it a try. It worked like a dream! I was able to get the exact temperatures needed to make several different kinds of candy without resorting to any mysterious chemistry!

MEASURING CUPS

Liquid measuring cups are available in various sizes; 1-cup and 2-cup sizes with a pouring spout are the most common. The measuring line is about 1" from the rim, so that the liquid being measured won't spill out.

Dry measuring cups are sold in sets of several graduated sizes. A level measure is even with the top rim. (See page 23 for measuring tips.)

MEASURING SPOONS

Measuring spoons are sold in sets of several graduated sizes. They are are used for both dry and wet ingredients.

OVEN

Be sure your oven is in good working order and the temperature regulator is accurate. When I started this book, I kept burning the recipes I was testing. I finally realized my oven's heat regulator was broken—I ended up buying a new stove!

Baking Tips

PREHEAT THE OVEN

All recipes that require baking must be set into a hot oven. Set the oven at the proper temperature and let it preheat while you are measuring and mixing the recipe ingredients. The recipe will not turn out properly if you put the baking pan into a cool oven and then turn the oven on.

MEASURE ACCURATELY

Accurate measuring is critical to the success of your baked goods. Different types of ingredients used in baking are measured in different ways. Here are the basics.

Flour. Spoon flour lightly into the appropriate-sized measuring cup up beyond the cup rim. Run a metal spatula blade straight across the top of the cup to level it off. Do not pour flour directly from the bag into the cup or tap or shake the cup to settle the flour.

Granulated Sugar. Pour granulated sugar directly into the measuring cup.

Brown Sugar. Pack brown sugar firmly into the measuring cup using the back of a spoon.

Shortening, Butter, or Margarine. Pack shortening, butter, or margarine into the appropriate-sized measuring cup and level off with a knife even with the cup rim. I prefer using butter or margarine in sticks as the measurements are marked right on the wrapper.

MIX COMPLETELY

Mix the ingredients together so that they are well blended and integrated, unless the recipe states otherwise. Do not overmix. Transfer the mixture into the baking pan using a rubber scraper to avoid waste.

WATCH YOUR TIME

Bake to the exact time specified in the recipe for a finished product that is neither underbaked nor burned. So you don't have to watch the clock, use an accurate timer with a loud bell or buzzer. Push a testing straw (sold at cookware stores) into cakes or loaves to test doneness. If the straw comes out with ingredients sticking to it, the item needs a few more minutes' baking time. If it comes out clean, the item is properly baked.

Wrapping Food for Gift-Giving

When you present a gift of food, be sure to choose suitable packaging. Soup, small cookies, snacks, and dessert toppings can be placed in attractive jars or containers. Pastries, bread, and bar desserts can be wrapped in aluminum foil, plastic wrap, or zip-lock bags. Wrapping the food is a must for preserving freshness and for protecting the sewn portion of your gift from damage or soil.

The items used to make the gift containers for the projects were purchased in craft supply and import stores. They include wreaths, baskets, a miniature bed, a serving tray, and a birdcage. It is my hope that you will be able to find similar items for making the projects in your area. Most craft supply stores buy from the same suppliers and thus carry just about the same stock. If you cannot find a certain item, ask the store manager if it can be ordered for you. Many craft supply stores are more than willing to help good customers. If you are unable to find the exact size item specified in the project, you may be able to adapt the directions. For example, you might add extra strips to the House and Heart Tray inset (page 87) to fit a tray with a larger opening.

Seasons

❧

*Nature's procession through the year brings renewed joy and warm
sentiments with the arrival of each of the seasons. Spring, Summer,
Winter, Fall—each is an occasion itself for creating these
timely—and tasty—gifts of love.*

"Friendship Ring"
Pizza Pan Cover and Pillow

After your friends polish off this delicious Apple Pizza, they can convert the versatile pan cover to a pillow—all they need to do is insert a round pillow form! The Friendship Ring appliqué is easy to sew and makes good use of fabric scraps. The green version features assorted 1930s fabrics found at a quilt sale. Covers shown are 12½" across, excluding trim; size will vary, depending on pan size used.

SUPPLIES

½ yard white/pastel print fabric
coordinating fabric scraps
1¼ yards 1½" white pregathered eyelet trim
1 yard ½" grosgrain ribbon
2 small safety pins

CUTTING GUIDE

17 assorted fabric A's
2 white/pastel print circles (use 12" pizza pan as pattern; see directions)

DIRECTIONS

Fold the white/pastel print fabric in half, right side in, and set the 12" pizza pan you will be using for the apple pizza on top. Measure and mark 1" beyond the pan edge all around. Pin the fabric layers together and cut on the marked line. You should have two large circles.

Place any two A shapes together, right sides facing. Sew one long straight edge between dots; press seam open. Join the remaining A shapes in the same way to form one large ring, as shown in Friendship Ring Diagram. Fold the inner circular and outer scalloped edges ¼" to the wrong side, baste in place, then steam-press. Center the ring on top of one of the large circles, right sides up. Appliqué in place (page 18). Remove basting threads.

Pin eyelet trim to the appliquéd circle, right sides facing and edges matching; fold and overlap the ends for a neat finish, trimming off any excess. Stitch ³⁄₁₆" from edge all around. Lay the second large circle on top, right sides facing and edges matching. Stitch through all three layers ¼" from edge, securing eyelet in the seam; leave a 7" opening for turning. Clip curve all around. Turn right side out.

To complete the cover, baste the opening closed with matching thread, taking loose stitches that can be easily removed later. Cut the ribbon in half, for two 18" pieces. Using two small safety pins, fasten one end of each ribbon to opposite edges of the cover back. Set the pan cover over the plastic-wrapped apple pizza and tie the ribbons on the underside to secure it.

Apple Pizza

Crust:
1¼ cups unsifted all-purpose flour
1 teaspoon salt
½ cup (1 stick) butter, chilled
1 cup shredded medium-flavored cheddar cheese
¼ cup ice water

12" pizza pan, greased

Topping:
½ cup brown sugar
½ cup granulated sugar
¼ cup unsifted all-purpose flour
¼ teaspoon salt
½ teaspoon ground cinnamon
⅛ teaspoon nutmeg
¼ cup butter, softened at room temperature
2 to 3 large Granny Smith green apples, peeled,
  cored, and thinly sliced
2 tablespoons freshly squeezed lemon juice

Preheat oven to 425°F. In a medium-sized bowl, mix 1¼ cups flour and 1 teaspoon salt. Using a pastry blender or two knives, cut in ½ cup butter until mixture resembles coarse meal. Add cheese and toss gently. Make a well in the center, then pour in ice water all at once. Stir quickly with a fork just enough to moisten all ingredients. Turn dough out onto a lightly floured board and form into a ball. Gently roll out dough from center to a ½-inch thickness, forming a 12-inch circle. Transfer dough circle to greased pizza pan, and pinch edges to form a ½-inch rim all around.

  In a small bowl, combine brown sugar, granulated sugar, ¼ cup flour, ¼ teaspoon salt, cinnamon, and nutmeg. Sprinkle half of the mixture evenly over the crust. Mix butter into remaining mixture with your fingers until crumbly, and set aside. Beginning at the outer edge of pastry, arrange apple slices in concentric rings, overlapping slices slightly. Sprinkle with lemon juice and remaining crumb mixture. Bake for 35 minutes, or until apples are tender.
Makes 10 to 12 servings.

Friendship Ring Diagram

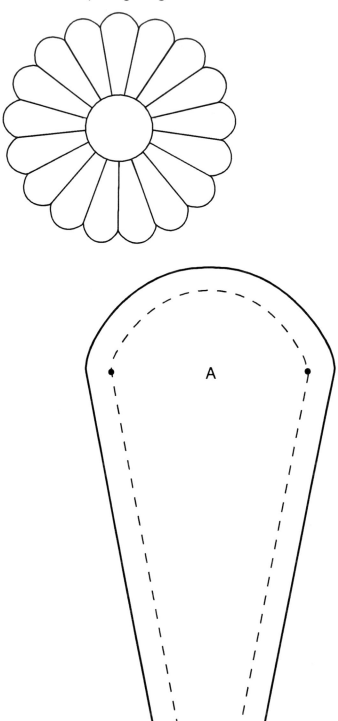

A

Sprinkling Can Cover
and Mini Wall Ornament

Like yesteryear's lunch pails, a metal watering can helps keep goodies like Shel's Famous Lemon Bars cool and moist. The protective April Showers cover fits on top and ties to the can handle at each side. Once the gift is delivered, the ribbon ties can be removed and the cover can be hung as a wall ornament. I've always loved the sunny yellow hollyhock pattern—this 1930s-style appliqué is sure to brighten even the rainiest of spring days. Cover is 6" across.

SUPPLIES

white metal sprinkling can, 6" diameter × 6" high
¼ yard white/light green print fabric
scraps of bright yellow, green, and white fabric
1⅓ yards ½" yellow picot-edged satin ribbon
⅝ yard yellow bias binding
1 skein each dark green, lavender, and deep purple embroidery floss
scrap of fiberfill batting
½" plastic crochet ring
2 small safety pins

CUTTING GUIDE

2 white/light green print background circles (do not cut until embroidery is completed; see directions)
1 yellow hollyhock flower A
1 white hollyhock center B
4 green hollyhock leaf C's
1 6½" fiberfill batting circle

DIRECTIONS

Trace the background circle (outer solid line of pattern) twice on right side of white/light green print fabric. Trace the words and vine design inside one of the circles. Place the fabric in an embroidery hoop (page 17). Using three strands floss in needle, embroider the words in deep purple backstitch, the vine in dark green backstitch, and the buds and pods in deep purple and lavender satin stitch.

Prepare yellow hollyhock A, white center B, and four green leaf C's for applique (page 18). Following the Appliqué Placement Diagram, arrange these six pieces on the center of the embroidered circle, slipping leaf edges under the hollyhock and placing the white center on top. Appliqué in place.

Cut out both circles. Place them together, wrong sides facing, and slip the batting circle in between. Line up the edges, then baste all around. Bind with yellow bias binding (page 19). Quilt around the hollyhock, center, and leaves in outline quilting (page 17).

Referring to the pattern for placement, sew the plastic crochet ring to the back of the cover at the O for a hanger. Cut the ribbon in half, for two 24" lengths. Fold each piece in half. Using two small safety pins, fasten the folded edge of each ribbon to the back of the cover at the ×'s. Place the wrapped lemon bars in the sprinkling can, place the cover on top, and tie the ribbon ends to the handle at each side.

Shel's Famous Lemon Bars

Crust:
2¼ cups all-purpose flour
¼ cup confectioners' sugar
1 cup (2 sticks) butter, melted

13" × 9" × 2" baking pan, ungreased

Topping:
4 large eggs
2 cups granulated sugar
1 tablespoon unsifted flour
2 teaspoons baking powder
7 tablespoons freshly squeezed lemon juice
confectioners' sugar

Preheat oven to 350°F. In a large mixing bowl, mix 2¼ cups flour, confectioners' sugar, and melted butter together with a wooden spoon until light yellow and crumbly. Press mixture into bottom of ungreased baking pan, and bake for 20 minutes. In a medium mixing bowl, mix eggs, sugar, flour, baking powder, and lemon juice together with a wooden spoon until light yellow and smooth. Pour over previously baked crust. Bake crust and topping 25 minutes, or until edges are brown and a baking straw inserted in center comes out clean. Remove from oven, let cool in pan for 10 minutes, then sprinkle top lightly with confectioners' sugar. Cut into 1½" × 3¼" bars using a sharp knife.
Makes 24 bars.

Appliqué Placement Diagram

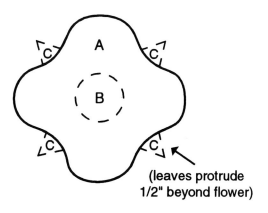

(leaves protrude
1/2" beyond flower)

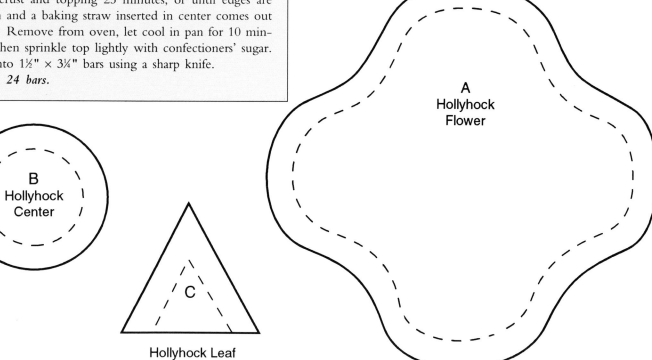

B
Hollyhock
Center

Hollyhock Leaf

A
Hollyhock
Flower

APRIL SHOWERS

BRING MAY FLOWERS

O = sew crochet ring to back
X = pin ribbons to back

Watermelon Picnic Basket and Napkin Set

Even if watermelons weren't one of today's most popular country motifs, they would still spell summer to me. For my summer picnic basket, I decorated a fabric panel and companion napkins with watermelon appliqués and miniature rickrack trim. Don't worry about getting the appliquéd design soiled when you take the basket on a picnic; you can easily remove it for washing, then reglue it to the basket front. Pack ice inside the basket around Rita's Ice Cream Pie for a quick hop to a friend's backyard picnic or barbeque. The watermelon panel fits a 9" × 14" × 7" basket; napkin is 16" × 16".

SUPPLIES

rectangular picnic basket 9" × 14" × 7" or larger; front panel must be at least 9" × 14"
1 yard white/red print fabric (makes 4 napkins)
⅜ yard white fabric
¼ yard green fabric
¼ yard red fabric
scrap of dark green fabric
red miniature rickrack: 1⅜ yards for basket plus 1⅞ yards for each napkin
1 skein each red, green, and black embroidery floss
glue gun

PICNIC BASKET CUTTING GUIDE

1 white fabric panel 9" × 14", or to fit basket front (see directions to measure; do not cut until embroidery and appliqué are completed)
1 green rind A
1 white rind B
1 red melon C (do not cut until seeds are embroidered; see directions)
2 dark green leaf D's (do not cut until veins are embroidered; see directions)

PICNIC BASKET DIRECTIONS

Measure your basket's front panel. Using a marking pen, draw a rectangle this size on right side of white fabric. Measure ¼" in from these four cutting lines and mark foldlines. Measure and mark the center point of each long edge. Trace the word PICNIC ¼" below one long foldline, aligning the center mark on the fabric with the center line on the pattern. Trace leaf, vine, tendrils, and watermelon placement line, reversing pattern to complete the design on the right side. Complete the C half-pattern (page 38). Trace C outline and 6 seeds on right side of red fabric. Trace 2 D leaves with veins on right side of dark green fabric.

Place the marked white fabric in an embroidery hoop (page 17). Using three strands floss in needle, embroider the word PICNIC in red chain stitch,

the vine in green chain stitch, and the vine tendrils in green backstitch. Embroider the seeds on red melon C in black satin stitch and the veins on both dark green leaves D in black backstitch Cut out C and D's on the solid lines.

Prepare the curved edges of green rind A, white rind B, red melon C, and dark green leaf D's for appliqué (page 18). Appliqué B to A so the green rind extends ½" below the white rind. Appliqué C to B so the white rind extends ½" below the red melon. Fold the long straight top edge of watermelon slice ¼" to wrong side, baste through all layers, and steam-press. Pin to the white panel, so top edge of melon touches the placement line. Appliqué around entire melon. Appliqué dark green leaves in place.

Cut out the white panel on the marked lines. Press the edges ¼" to the wrong side as marked. Hand-sew miniature rickrack around the edge, so rickrack points extend beyond fold. Hot-glue block to basket front.

NAPKIN CUTTING GUIDE

For each napkin, cut:
1 white/red print fabric square 17" × 17"
1 green rind A
1 white rind B
1 red melon C (do not cut until seed is
embroidered; see directions)

NAPKIN DIRECTIONS

To hem fabric square, press raw edges ¼" to wrong side twice, then topstitch ³⁄₁₆" from outer fold through all layers. Hand-sew miniature rickrack around the edge, concealing topstitching.

Trace C outline and 1 seed on right side of red fabric. Place red melon C in embroidery hoop (page 17). Using three strands floss in needle, embroider the seed in black satin stitch.

Cut out C on the solid lines. Prepare the curved edges of white rind B and red melon C for appliqué. Appliqué B to A so the green rind extends ½" beyond the white rind. Appliqué C to B so the white rind extends ½" beyond the red melon. Using the paper template method for hand-appliqué (page 18), fold edges of watermelon slice ¼" to wrong side. Baste, steam-press, then remove the basting thread and template. Appliqué to corner of napkin as shown in photograph.

Rita's Ice Cream Pie

1 cup evaporated milk
¾ cup semisweet chocolate chips
1 cup mini marshmallows
¼ teaspoon salt
1 11-oz. box vanilla wafers
¼ gallon mint chocolate chip ice cream, slightly
softened
1 8-oz. container non-dairy whipped topping
¼ cup milk chocolate shavings

9" pie plate

In a medium saucepan, combine evaporated milk, chocolate chips, mini marshmallows, and salt, and cook over medium heat, stirring until chocolate chips and marshmallows are melted and all ingredients are well blended. Remove from heat and let cool. Line bottom and sides of pie plate with vanilla wafers. Spread a thin layer of ice cream over bottom layer of vanilla wafers. Spoon some of the cooled chocolate-marshmallow mixture evenly over ice cream. Continue adding ice cream and mixture alternately in layers until pie plate is filled. Top with a generous amount of non-dairy whipped topping and sprinkle with chocolate shavings. Freeze until solid. Remove from freezer and let stand 10 minutes before serving. Slice into pie-shaped wedges with a sharp knife.
Makes 6 generous servings.

WATERMELON BASKET COVER

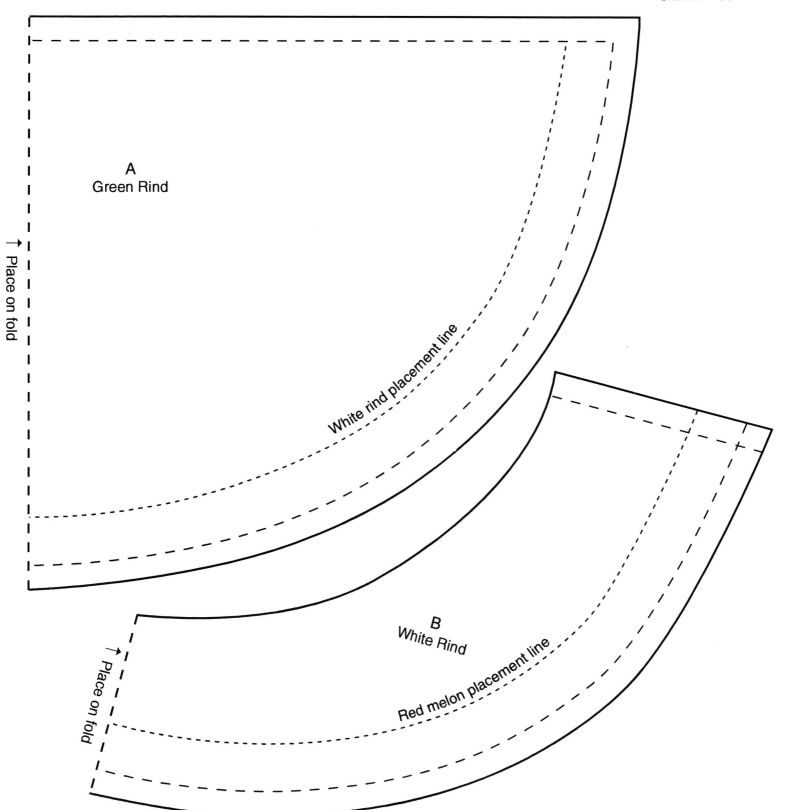

A
Green Rind

→ Place on fold

White rind placement line

B
White Rind

→ Place on fold

Red melon placement line

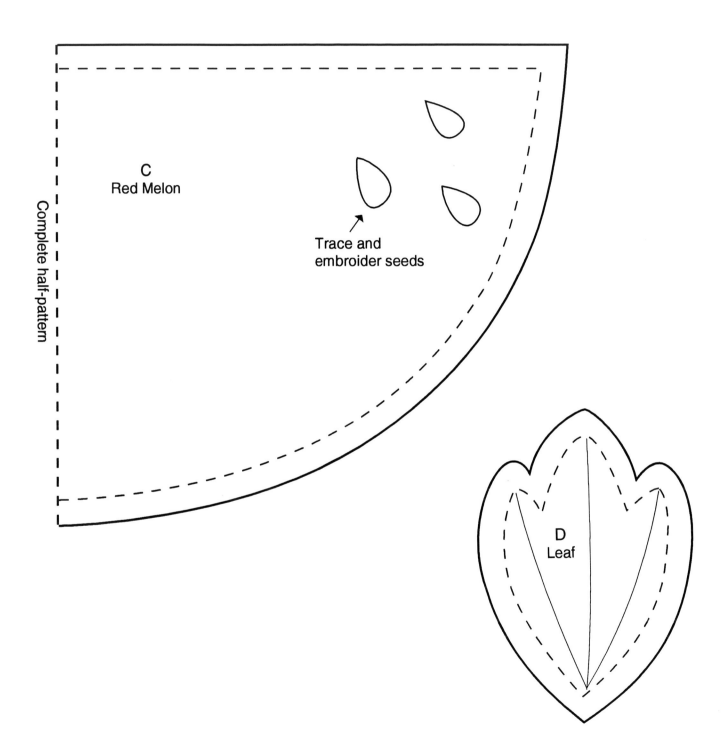

Complete half-pattern

C
Red Melon

Trace and
embroider seeds

D
Leaf

WATERMELON SLICE NAPKIN

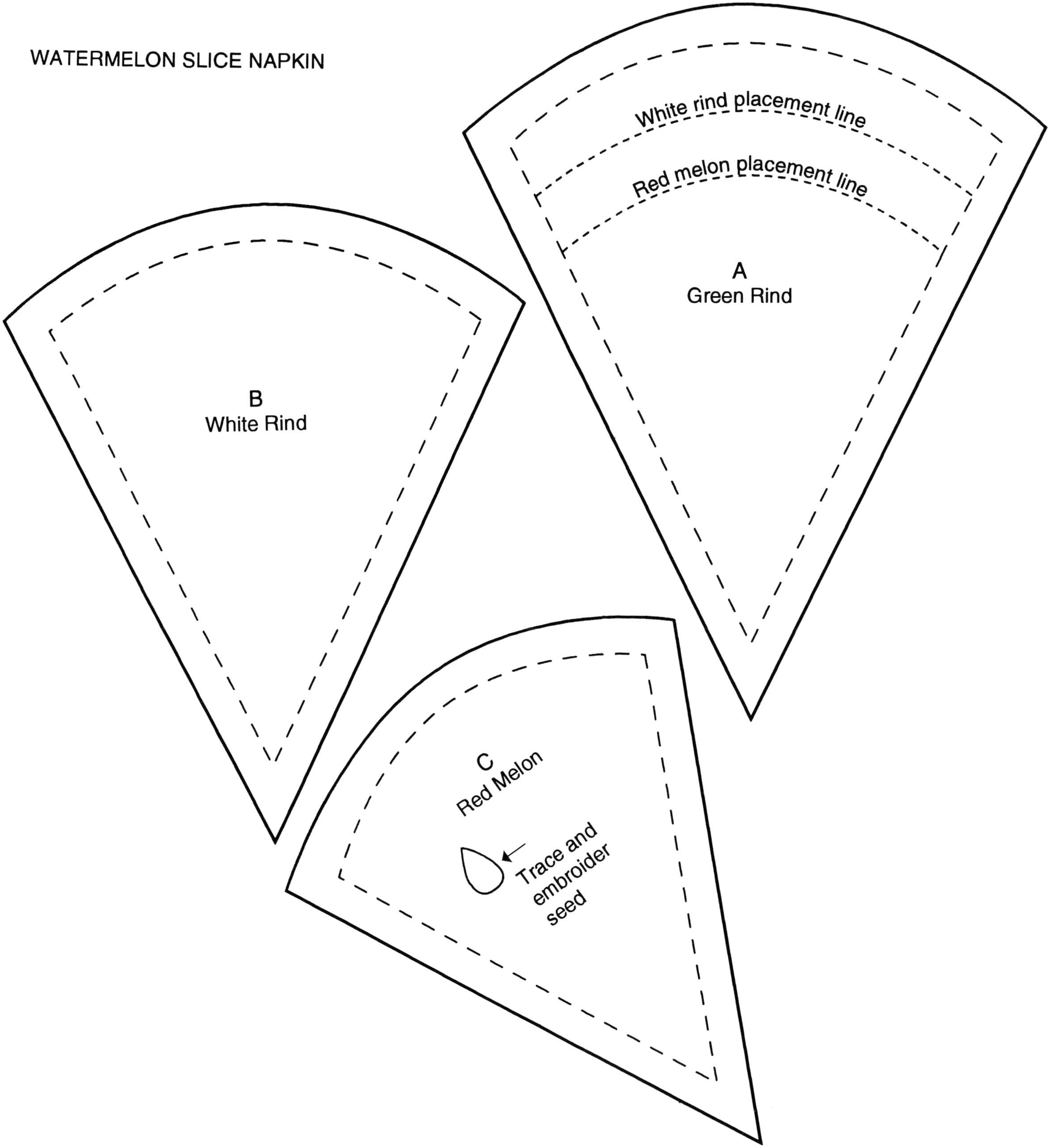

White rind placement line

Red melon placement line

A
Green Rind

B
White Rind

C
Red Melon

Trace and embroider seed

Sailboat Tote

Growing up in San Diego, I loved to go down to the bay and watch the sailboats. This red and white tote features a patchwork sailboat in the center and prairie point trim around the top edge. It is roomy enough for a towel and swimsuit. For gift-giving, I pack the tote with Phyllo *Cerisaie*, or "cherry garden." This scrumptious dessert was created by my friend Alma Galgiani just for this book. Tote is 16" × 16", excluding trim and handles.

SUPPLIES

1 yard dark red/white print fabric
¼ yard medium red check fabric
¼ yard dark red fabric
⅛ yard white fabric
fiberfill batting

CUTTING GUIDE

For sailboat block (make 1):
  6 dark red A's
  6 white A's
  6 white B's
  1 white C
  1 dark red C
For each corner block (make 4):
  4 dark red B's
  4 white B's
  2 white D's
Additional pieces for tote:
  4 dark red/white print E squares 4½" × 4½"
  2 medium red check F strips 2½" × 12½"
  2 medium red check G strips 2½" × 16½"
  approximately 22 dark red H's
  2 dark red/white print I strips 3½" × 15"

1 dark red/white print back 16½" × 16½"
2 dark red/white print linings 16½" × 16½"
2 fiberfill batting squares 16½" × 16½"
2 fiberfill batting strips 1½" × 15"

DIRECTIONS

Make one sailboat patchwork block following Diagram 1. Sew dark red A's and white A's together in pairs for 6 A/A squares (a). Sew white B's together in two groups of three, then sew an A/A square to end of each strip in mirror image (b). Sew 4 A/A squares together to make one square, positioning so dark triangles point towards lower left (c). Sew a white C to the top of the block and a red C to the bottom of the block (d). Sew A/B strips to sides to complete the sailboat block (e).

  Make four corner patchwork blocks following Diagram 2. For each block, sew dark red B's and white B's together in pairs for 4 B/B rectangles (a). Sew B/B rectangles together in pairs so adjacent fabrics contrast (b). Sew each pieced B square to a white D (c). Sew B/D pieces together to complete the block (d).

  Assemble the tote front following Diagram 3. Sew two B/D blocks to each side of a dark red/white print E so dark red B's ascend to top outer corners (a). Make a second identical strip, then turn 180 degrees so dark red B's descend to bottom outer corners. Sew two remaining E's to each side of sailboat block (b). Sew the three strips together, with the sailboat block in the center. Frame block by sewing two red check F's to top and bottom edges, then two red check G's to side edges. Tote front should measure 16½" × 16½" (c).

Lay tote front on top of a batting square, right side up, and baste with long, loose stitches. Quilt around boat shape, white B's in the corner blocks, white D's, and strips F and G in outline quilting. Using quilter's tape or a marking pen, mark three vertical lines 1" apart on the E blocks above and below sailboat and three horizontal lines 1" apart on the E blocks to right and left of sailboat. Quilt on marked lines. Remove all basting threads.

Place tote front and back together, right sides facing and edges matching. Place remaining batting square on tote back, and pin all around. Stitch side and bottom edges together ¼" from edges, catching batting in seam; leave top edge open. Trim batting close to stitching, then turn right side out. Sew linings together in same manner; do not turn. Press top edge of lining ¼" to wrong side.

Make prairie point chain following Diagram 4. Fold each H in half diagonally (a), then in half again, for a triangle shape; steam-press to hold creases (b). Pin points together, setting each new point about ¼" into fold of previous point. Stitch ¼" from edge to join points in a chain about 33" long (c). Finished length may vary, depending on depth of overlaps; if necessary, add a few more points. Pin finished chain around top of tote, raw edges matching; slip last point into first point for a neat finish. Stitch ¼" from edges.

Make handles following Diagram 5. Press one long edge of each I strip ¼" to wrong side (a). Lay on a flat surface, wrong side up, and center batting strip on top. Fold each I strip around batting strip, overlapping raw edge ¼" at center; pin in place (b). Topstitch along folded edge through all layers, securing fabric to batting. Pin handles, right sides facing and raw edges matching, to top edge of tote front and back 5½" in from side seams. Stitch ¼" from edges over previous stitching. Trim batting close to stitching. Press tote top edge to wrong side along stitching line, so prairie points and handles pop up.

Insert the lining into the bag between the front and back batting, matching seams and folds. Hand-sew the lining to the tote along the top inside edge, concealing prairie point machine stitching.

Alma's Phyllo *Cerisaie* (Cherry Garden)

  1 tablespoon butter or margarine, melted
10 sheets phyllo pastry dough
  1 21-oz. can cherry pie filling
 ¼ teaspoon chocolate raspberry flavoring
  2 crushed cardamom seeds
 ¼ teaspoon ground coffee
 ½ teaspoon almond extract
confectioners' sugar
9-oz. jar Maraschino cherries
toothpicks with red decorative tops

8" square glass baking dish

Preheat oven to 350°F. Using a pastry brush, brush a small amount of melted butter onto the bottom and sides of baking dish, just enough to coat. Following package directions for handling phyllo dough, place 5 sheets of dough into the baking dish to line bottom and sides and double over ends. Using a sharp knife, cut off excess dough even with dish sides and set cuttings aside. Brush surface of dough with melted butter. In a medium-sized bowl, combine cherry pie filling, chocolate raspberry flavoring, cardamom, coffee, and almond extract, and mix well. Pour mixture evenly over phyllo layers and spread to edges. Distribute leftover cuttings evenly across top. Layer remaining 5 sheets of phyllo, folded double, on top, and cut off excess to fit. Brush top with the remaining melted butter. Using a sharp knife, score the top layer of pastry into diamonds 2 inches wide. Bake for 35 to 40 minutes, or until golden brown. Let cool thoroughly in pan, then sprinkle confectioners' sugar lightly across the top. Cut into pieces along scored lines. Top each piece with a Maraschino cherry secured by a toothpick.
Makes 8 servings.

Diagram 1
Sailboat Block

 (a)

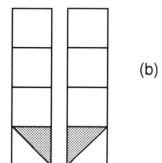 (b)

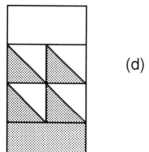 (c)

(d)

Diagram 2
Corner Blocks

 (a)

 (b)

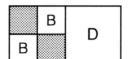 (c)

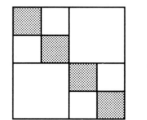 (d)

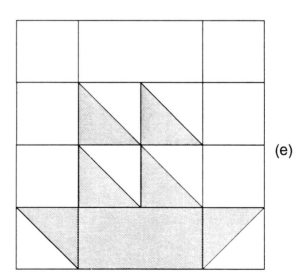 (e)

Diagram 3
Tote Front Assembly

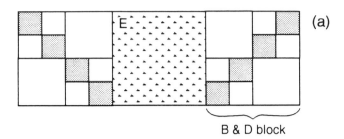

(a)

B & D block

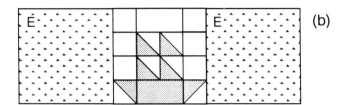

(b)

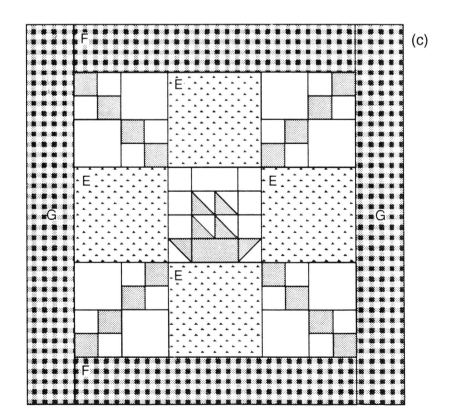

(c)

Diagram 4
Step-by-step Prairie Points Edging

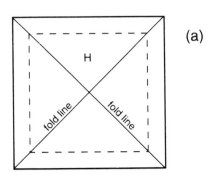

(a)

(b)

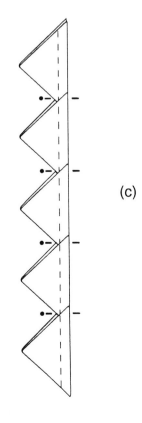

(c)

Diagram 5
Handles

(a)

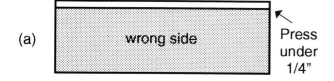

wrong side

Press
under
1/4"

(b)

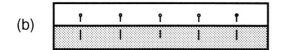

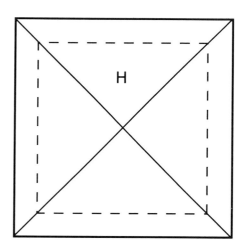

H

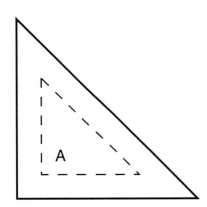

A

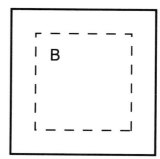

B

C

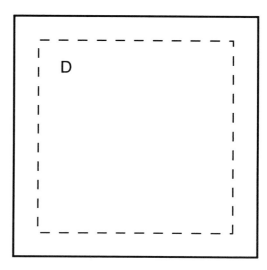

D

Loaf Pan Cover with Acorn Tag

This cozy quilted cover ties around a small loaf of home-baked Zucchini Bread. When the ties are removed, the cover converts to a practical hot pad to slip under casseroles or hot plates. Autumn colors and an embroidered acorn tag make this gift a welcome contribution at cool-weather suppers and gatherings. The bread is extra-tasty served alongside Robin's Hearty Vegetable Soup (see page 52). Loaf cover is 6½" × 13½"; tag is 2¼" × 3¾".

LOAF PAN COVER SUPPLIES

Note: The rust and black covers shown in photograph are variations of the same design. Supplies and directions below are for rust cover. They can be adapted to make the black version.

¼ yard cream print fabric
¼ yard very dark rust print fabric
⅛ yard dark rust print fabric (increase yardage for seamless bias binding)
scrap of medium rust print fabric
1 yard ½" rust grosgrain ribbon
scrap of fiberfill batting

LOAF PAN COVER CUTTING GUIDE

For each patchwork block (make 2):
12 cream print A's
6 medium rust print A's
6 dark rust print A's
2 very dark rust print B's
2 very dark rust print C's
Additional pieces for cover:
1 very dark rust print D
1 cream print lining 6½" × 13"

1⅛ yards dark rust print bias binding (see page 19 to make binding)
1 fiberfill batting rectangle 6½" × 13½"

LOAF PAN COVER DIRECTIONS

Make two patchwork blocks following Diagram 1. For each block, sew 6 dark rust print A's and 6 cream print A's together in pairs for 6 A/A squares (a). Sew 6 medium rust print A's and 6 cream print A's together in pairs for 6 A/A squares (b). Sew 12 A/A squares together in rows of four, alternating both colors and position of diagonal seam across row (c). Sew three rows together. Frame each finished block by sewing 2 very dark rust print B's to short edges, then 2 very dark rust print C's to long edges. Join each block to long edges of very dark rust print D. Piece should measure 6½" × 13½".

Place the patchwork cover and lining together, wrong sides facing, and slip the batting in between. Line up the edges, then baste through all layers horizontally and vertically in long, loose stitches. Quilt cream print A's, around the two large pieced A blocks, and along the edges of D in outline quilting. Bind with dark rust print bias binding (page 19). Remove basting threads.

Cut ribbon in half, for two 18" pieces. Fold one end of each piece down ¼" and tack to short edges of cover on wrong side. To use cover as a hot pad, pick out stitches and remove ribbons.

BAKED
JUST FOR
YOU!

ACORN TAG SUPPLIES

scrap of muslin
⅓ yard dark green bias binding
5" piece ¼" dark green satin ribbon
1 skein each rust, gold, orange, medium green, and dark green embroidery floss

ACORN TAG CUTTING GUIDE

2 muslin tags (do not cut until embroidery is completed; see directions)

ACORN TAG DIRECTIONS

Trace the tag outline twice on right side of muslin. Trace the words acorn, and leaves inside one tag. Place the fabric in an embroidery hoop (page 17). Using two strands floss in needle, embroider the words in dark green backstitch, the acorn in gold satin stitch, the acorn cap in rust satin stitch, the acorn leaves in medium and dark green satin stitch, and the stray leaf in orange satin stitch. Using one strand floss, embroider the leaf veins in contrasting backstitch.

Cut out both tags. Place them together, wrong sides facing, and bind the edges with dark green bias binding (page 19). Fold the ribbon in half and tack to wrong side of tag at position marked by × on pattern.

Zucchini Bread

1½ medium zucchinis, shredded
1½ teaspoons salt
5 large eggs
2 tablespoons milk
4 tablespoons vegetable oil
½ cup grated Parmesan cheese
1 tablespoon garlic powder
1 teaspoon dried basil
¼ teaspoon pepper
3 tablespoons onion, finely chopped
1 cup unsifted all-purpose flour
1 tablespoon baking powder

6" x 3¾" x 2" foil loaf pan, greased and floured

Preheat oven to 375°F. Toss the zucchini and salt together in a medium-sized bowl, then let stand in a colander for 5 minutes, or until liquid drains off. Place zucchini between paper towels and squeeze with your fingers to eliminate as much excess moisture as possible. In a medium-sized bowl, whisk eggs, milk, oil, cheese, garlic powder, basil, and pepper until well blended. Add the zucchini and onion and mix well. In a separate small bowl, stir the flour with the baking powder. Add to the zucchini mixture and stir just until evenly moist. Pour mixture into greased and floured pan and spread evenly out to edges. Bake for 45 minutes, or until a testing straw comes out clean. Let cool in pan. *Makes 1 small loaf.*

Piecing Diagram

 (a)

 (b)

 (c)

Key:

 Cream Print

 Medium Print

 Dark Print

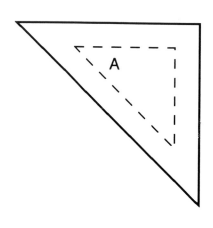

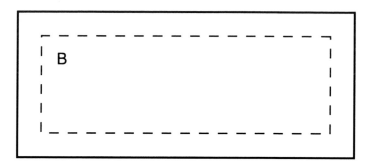

Pumpkin Jar Topper

A doily-trimmed jar topper, wheat sprigs, and a quilted orange pumpkin make a special fall presentation for your favorite homemade soup. My friend Robin Page loves to serve soup year-round, and she enjoys concocting new recipes for her family to try. She developed her original Hearty Vegetable Soup especially for this book. Fabric topper is 13" × 13", excluding trim.

SUPPLIES

2-quart glass canning jar with 4½"-diameter
  screw-on top
½ yard light brown pindot fabric
scrap of orange print fabric
1½ yards ¾" ecru flat eyelet trim
⅔ yard ⅝" fall plaid paper ribbon
9" round ecru crocheted doily
scrap of fiberfill batting
4 wheat tips
two ½" Velcro® dots
glue gun

CUTTING GUIDE

2 orange print pumpkins
1 fiberfill batting pumpkin without seam allowance
1 light brown pindot square 13½" × 13½"

DIRECTIONS

Trace quilting lines onto orange print pumpkins. Place pumpkins together, right sides facing. Stitch all around, leaving an opening at bottom for turning. Clip corners and curves; clip in at stem base as marked. Turn right side out. Insert batting pumpkin into opening and maneuver so it fills out the shape, including stem. Sew opening closed, making tiny stitches. Quilt on three lines, as indicated on pattern.

Press edges of light brown pindot square ¼" to wrong side twice. Pin eyelet trim around edge on wrong side, so scalloping extends beyond fold. Topstitch close to edge through all layers. Center doily on top of cover and tack in place with matching thread.

Screw lid on jar. Center fabric cover on top and secure with a rubber band. Cut a length of plaid paper ribbon to go around jar lid once plus 1½". Fold short ends of ribbon ½" to one side and hot-glue in place. Overlap folded ends by ½". Sandwich a Velcro® dot fastener (do not separate) in between and hot-glue in place. Tie remaining ribbon into a small bow, trim off excess, and hot-glue to front of pumpkin at base of stem. Hot-glue wheat tips to back of pumpkin, so they emerge at sides of stem. Hot-glue second Velcro® dot (do not separate) between back of pumpkin stem and midpoint of jar ribbon.

To assemble the gift, fill the jar with soup and screw on the cover. Center the fabric cover on top. Undo the ribbon Velcro® fastener. Fit the ribbon around the jar lid and fabric cover, and press the Velcro® dots together at the back.

Robin's Hearty Vegetable Soup

 3   medium zucchinis
 3   medium carrots
 3   medium potatoes
 1   bunch of celery
 2   small onions
 1   9-oz. box frozen green peas
 1   9-oz. box frozen cut green beans
 1   9-oz. box frozen corn
 1   46-oz. can V-8 juice
 1   20-oz. can chopped tomatoes in juice
2½ cups water
 ¼   cup molasses
 1   tablespoon salt
 1   teaspoon pepper
 2   teaspoons chili powder
 1   teaspoon dried oregano
 ½   teaspoon chopped basil leaves
10   garlic cloves, peeled and pushed through a
      garlic press
Parmesan cheese, for garnish

Wash zucchinis and peel carrots and potatoes. Slice zucchinis and carrots   into ¼-inch-thick coins. Cut potatoes into 2-inch cubes. Finely chop celery and onions. Place all ingredients except cheese in a large pot. Bring to a boil, then reduce heat and simmer for 1½ hours, stirring occasionally. To serve, ladle into bowls, then sprinkle with Parmesan cheese.
Makes 1 gallon, or 16 8-oz servings.

Note: To speed preparation, first five ingredients may be sliced or chopped in a food processor. Soup can be made into "Albondigas" type by adding precooked meatballs during last 10 minutes of simmering.

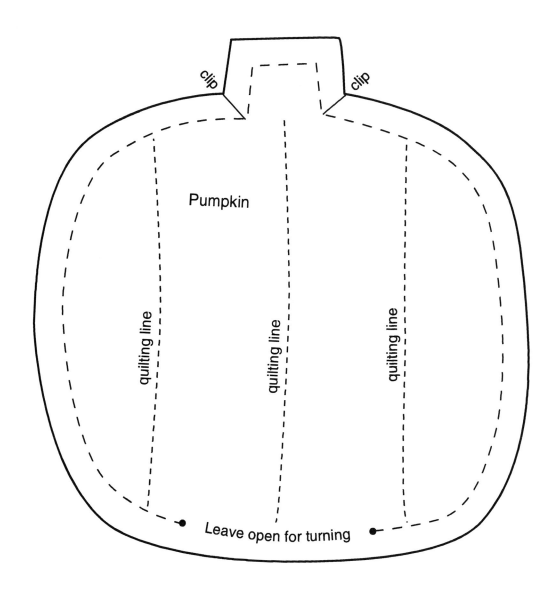

clip

clip

Pumpkin

quilting line

quilting line

quilting line

Leave open for turning

Country Doll
and Miniature Quilt

When I was a girl, I lined up all my dolls at the foot of my bed every night so I could choose one to take to bed with me. Those childhood dolls are long gone, but I have slowly been building a new collection of handmade dolls. I designed this cloth doll with doll lovers like me in mind. For gift-giving, lay the doll in a basket on a bed of excelsior, add wrapped Gingerbread Quilt Cookies alongside, and tuck the matching doll quilt over the top. Doll is 15" high; quilt is 13" × 13".

DOLL SUPPLIES

⅓ yard muslin
1 skein each black, brown, peach, and coral embroidery floss
1 skein medium brown wool mohair yarn
¼ yard ¹⁄₁₆" peach satin ribbon
ornamental flower for hair
blue fabric paint and brush
fiberfill
glue gun (optional)

DOLL CUTTING GUIDE

2 muslin doll head/body pieces (do not cut until embroidery is completed; see directions)
4 muslin arms
4 muslin legs

DOLL DIRECTIONS

Trace two doll head/bodies on right side of muslin. Trace face details and hairline inside one outline. Place fabric in embroidery hoop (page 17). Using two strands floss in needle, embroider a brown iris, black pupil, peach cheeks, and coral lips in satin stitch. Using one strand black floss in needle, embroider eye outline, lashes, eyebrow, and nose in backstitch. Cut out both head/body pieces on marked lines. Place pieces together, right sides facing, and sew edges together, leaving openings for arms and legs as indicated on pattern. Clip in at neck. Turn right side out.

Trace shoe guide on two legs and line for shoe back on two legs. Paint shoe area of muslin legs with blue paint. Let dry thoroughly. Sew arms and legs together in pairs, right sides facing; leave short straight edges open. Clip curves and turn right side out.

Stuff arms, legs, and head/body firmly with fiberfill. Insert arms into "sockets" and pin so no raw edges show. Hand-sew arms to body. Insert legs into "sockets," making sure feet face forward, and pin in place. Sew as for arms. Wrap quilting thread tightly around middle torso several times to nip in and form the waist; tie thread ends securely. Wrap thread in same manner around ends of arms to form wrists; tie off.

Attach hair following Doll Hair Diagram. Cut mohair wool yarn into approximately forty 16" strands. Using a large embroidery needle, "sew" each strand into the head at the hairline, pulling

yarn through until ends are even (a). Proceed until entire hairline is covered; you do not need to tie off ends. To make a curl, wrap a 10" length of yarn around a pencil. Using a needle and matching thread, hand-sew the loops together along one edge (b). Sew the curl to the hairline so hand stitches are against the head (c). Repeat until curls cover entire hairline. Take up a few strands of hair from ear area of hairline and bring them to the top of the head. Twist into a topknot and secure with a few small stitches (d). Turn doll around and trim long locks evenly across back below shoulder line (e). To match style in photograph, twist loose hair into a bun at nape of neck and secure with a glue gun or a few small stitches (f).

DRESS SUPPLIES

⅜ yard dark peach fabric
¼ yard ¾" white eyelet trim
three small snaps

DRESS CUTTING GUIDE

4 dark peach dress pieces (extend pattern at lower edge; see directions)

DRESS DIRECTIONS

To complete dress pattern, trace both sections, then tape lower extension to bottom edge of dress. Use extended pattern to cut 4 pieces. Place pieces together in pairs, right sides facing. Sew long straight edges together, leaving open above × on one set for dress back. Press open edges of center back ¼" to wrong side.

Place dress front and back together, right sides facing, and sew upper arm seam. Open out dress. Pin eyelet trim to neck edge, right sides facing and edges matching. Sew through both layers ¼" from edge; clip curves. Press lower edge of each sleeve ¼" to the wrong side and topstitch.

Refold dress right side in. Stitch each underarm seam from wrist to lower edge. Press skirt edge ¼", then ⅜" to wrong side; topstitch ³⁄₁₆" from edge to secure.

To finish, turn ends of eyelet trim to inside and tack in place. Separate the snaps into three male and three female pieces. Referring to pattern, sew three male snap halves to inside of left dress back; sew three female snaps in corresponding positions to outside of right dress back. Put dress on doll and fasten snaps to secure.

APRON AND QUILT SUPPLIES

⅛ yard muslin
½ yard cream print fabric
⅛ yard blue plaid fabric
⅛ yard blue print fabric
⅛ yard peach print fabric
⅛ yard coral fabric
3½ yards ¼" peach satin ribbon
1½ yards white eyelet beading (for ¼" ribbon insertion) with attached ½" eyelet ruffle along one edge
fiberfill batting

APRON CUTTING GUIDE

4 blue plaid A's
4 blue print A's
2 blue plaid B's
8 muslin C's
2 cream print bibs
2 cream print waistbands
2 cream print top ties
1 cream print skirt 8" x 12"
two 9" lengths peach satin ribbon

APRON DIRECTIONS

Make four pieced blocks for apron, referring to Quilt Diagram 1. Sew blue plaid A's to blue print A's together in pairs for 4 A/A rectangles. Sew rectangles together in pairs for 4 pieced A blocks (a). Sew four muslin C's to each blue plaid B to make 2 blue diamond blocks (b). Prepare blocks for appliqué (page 18).

Fold long edges of ties ¼" to wrong side and press. Fold in half lengthwise, matching folded edges, and machine-stitch to secure. Pin tie ends to edge of bib front at positions marked by ×'s on pattern. Place bib front and back together, right sides facing and edges matching. Stitch sides and top, catching ties in seam; leave lower edge open. Turn right side out. Appliqué a blue diamond block to bib front, following placement lines on pattern.

Press 8" edges of cream print skirt ¼" to wrong side twice, then topstitch 3/16" from outer fold through all layers. Press one 12" edge ¼", then 1" to wrong side. Hem by hand, making tiny stitches. Fold skirt in half, shorter edges matching, and mark center with pins. Open skirt out again. Center a blue diamond block on point on skirt front ½" above hem and pin in place. Pin two pieced A blocks on point at each side, so blocks just touch. Appliqué all three blocks in place.

Machine-baste two parallel rows 3/16" and 5/16" from skirt's top raw edge. Pull bobbin threads to gather skirt. Place waistbands together, right sides facing and edges matching. Sew two short edges and one long edge together. Clip corners and turn right side out. Fold raw edges ¼" to inside and press. Pin one raw edge of waistband to gathered edge of apron skirt, right sides facing; adjust gathers so they fall at the side, not front, of the skirt. Sew waistband to skirt ¼" from edge along pressed foldline—stitching should fall between the two gathering rows. Turn waistband up. Hand-sew folded edge to skirt top on wrong side, concealing raw edges.

Press lower edge of bib ¼" toward front. Hand-sew to inside edge of waistband at center front. Tack tie ends to inside waistband at back, turning ends under so they don't show. To make waist ties, sew 9" peach ribbons to ends of waistband on wrong side.

QUILT CUTTING GUIDE

24 blue plaid A's
24 cream print A's
5 blue print B's
8 peach print B's
52 muslin C's
2 coral D strips 1" × 10½"
2 coral E strips 1" × 11½"
2 cream print F strips 1½" × 11½"
2 cream print G strips 1½" × 13"
1 cream print back 13½" × 13½"
1 fiberfill batting square 13" × 13"
4 27" lengths peach satin ribbon

QUILT DIRECTIONS

Assemble quilt top following Diagram 1. Sew blue plaid A's and cream print A's together in pairs for 24 A/A rectangles. Sew rectangles together in pairs for 12 pieced A blocks (a). Sew 4 muslin C's to each B to make 5 blue diamond blocks (b) and 8 peach diamond blocks (c). Arrange A blocks and B/C blocks alternately in five rows. Make two rows with blue diamonds on the outside and a peach diamond in the center (d). Make one row with peach diamonds on the outside and a blue diamond in the center. Make two rows with pieced A blocks on the outside and in the center and peach diamond blocks in between (e). Sew the rows together so blue diamonds appear in the corners and the center. Frame the block by sewing 2 coral D strips to the top and bottom edges, 2 coral

E strips to the side edges, 2 cream print F strips to the top and bottom edges, and 2 cream print G strips to the side edges. Finished quilt top should measure 13½" × 13½".

Place quilt top and back together, right sides facing and edges matching. Sew around entire quilt, leaving a 4" opening in the middle of one straight edge for turning. Clip corners and turn to right side. Insert batting into opening and maneuver so it fills out into the corners. Sew opening closed. Baste through all layers horizontally and vertically with long, loose stitches. Quilt cream print A's, peach print B's, and cream print F/G border in outline quilting.

To finish quilt, hand-sew white eyelet beading to outer edge of quilt front, mitering trim to turn corners; allow eyelet ruffle to extend off edge of quilt. Run peach ribbons through beading on each side of quilt. Tie ends together in bows at corners, then trim ends diagonally.

Gingerbread Quilt Cookies

½ cup butter, softened at room temperature
2 tablespoons light molasses
2 tablespoons light corn syrup
1 large egg
1 teaspoon white vinegar
1 teaspoon ground ginger
1 teaspoon ground cloves
½ teaspoon ground cinnamon
1¼ cups granulated sugar
2 cups presifted all-purpose flour
1 teaspoon baking soda
confectioners' sugar

cookie sheets, ungreased

Frosting:
⅓ cup semisweet chocolate chips
1 tablespoon butter
1 tablespoon milk

Preheat oven to 325°F. In a medium mixing bowl, cream softened butter, molasses, and corn syrup together until smooth. Mix in the egg, vinegar, spices, and sugar, beating until well blended. Gradually add the flour and baking soda, mixing until well combined. With slightly damp hands, form dough into 2-inch balls and set on ungreased cookie sheets about 2 inches apart. Flatten and shape each ball into a 3¼" × 3¼" square. Bake for 15 minutes, or until brown; to avoid brittleness, do not overbake. Set on wire racks to cool; cookies must be thoroughly cool before frosting.

Place chocolate, butter, and milk in a small saucepan over low heat and stir until chocolate and butter are melted and ingredients are well blended. Set aside and let cool to room temperature. Set the Lover's Knot template on top of a cookie. Using a pastry brush, brush the cooled chocolate mixture over the template cutout design. Lift the template immediately and allow the chocolate frosting to set. When frosting is firm, wrap each cookie in plastic wrap.
Makes 12 large cookies.

Note: Cut template for frosting before you begin. Photocopy or trace the Lover's Knot pattern and outline, then tape the copy to lightweight cardboard. Cut on the marked lines with a craft knife and remove the cutout shapes to make template.

Doll's Hair Diagram

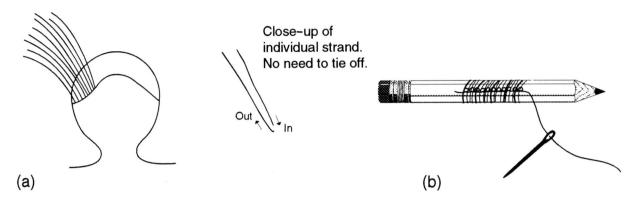

(a)

Close-up of individual strand. No need to tie off.

Out In

(b)

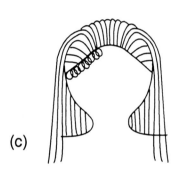

(c)

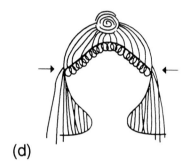

(d)

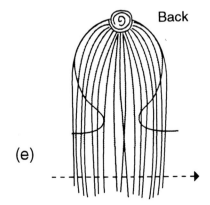

Back

(e)

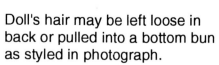

Doll's hair may be left loose in back or pulled into a bottom bun as styled in photograph.

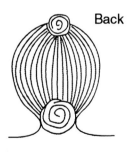

Back

(f)

Secure bottom bun with glue gun or needle and thread.

Diagram 1 (a)

Block #1

 (b)

 (c)

Block #2

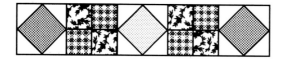 (d)

 (e)

 (f)

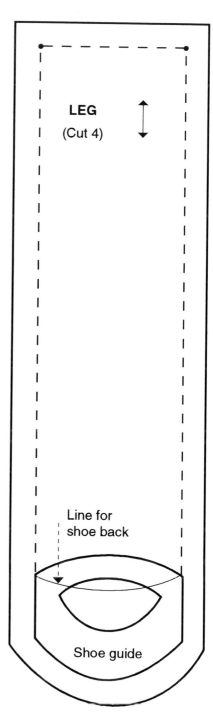

LEG

(Cut 4)

Line for
shoe back

Shoe guide

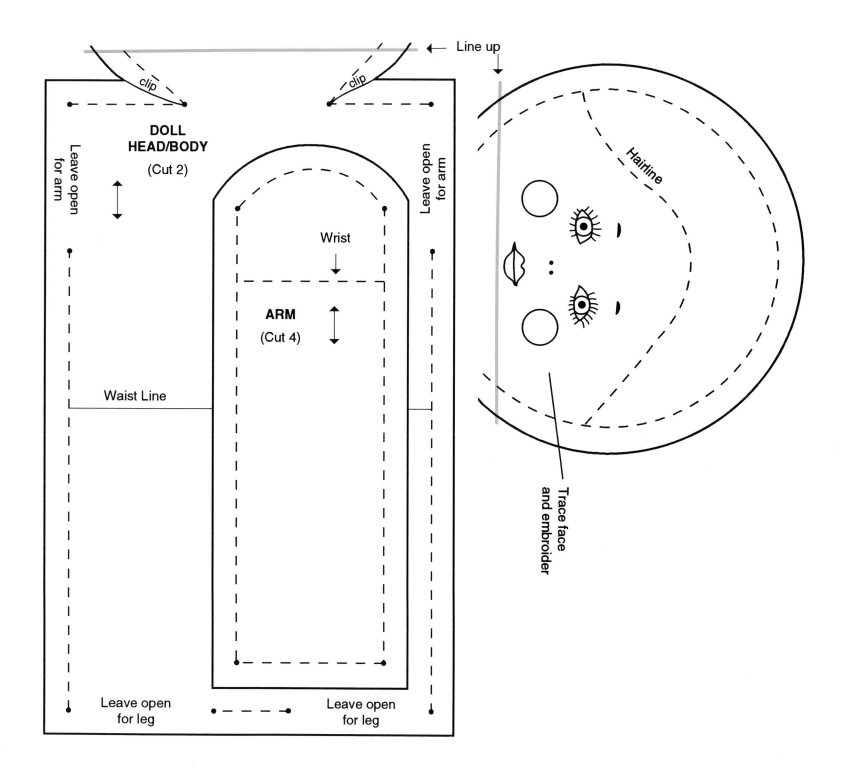

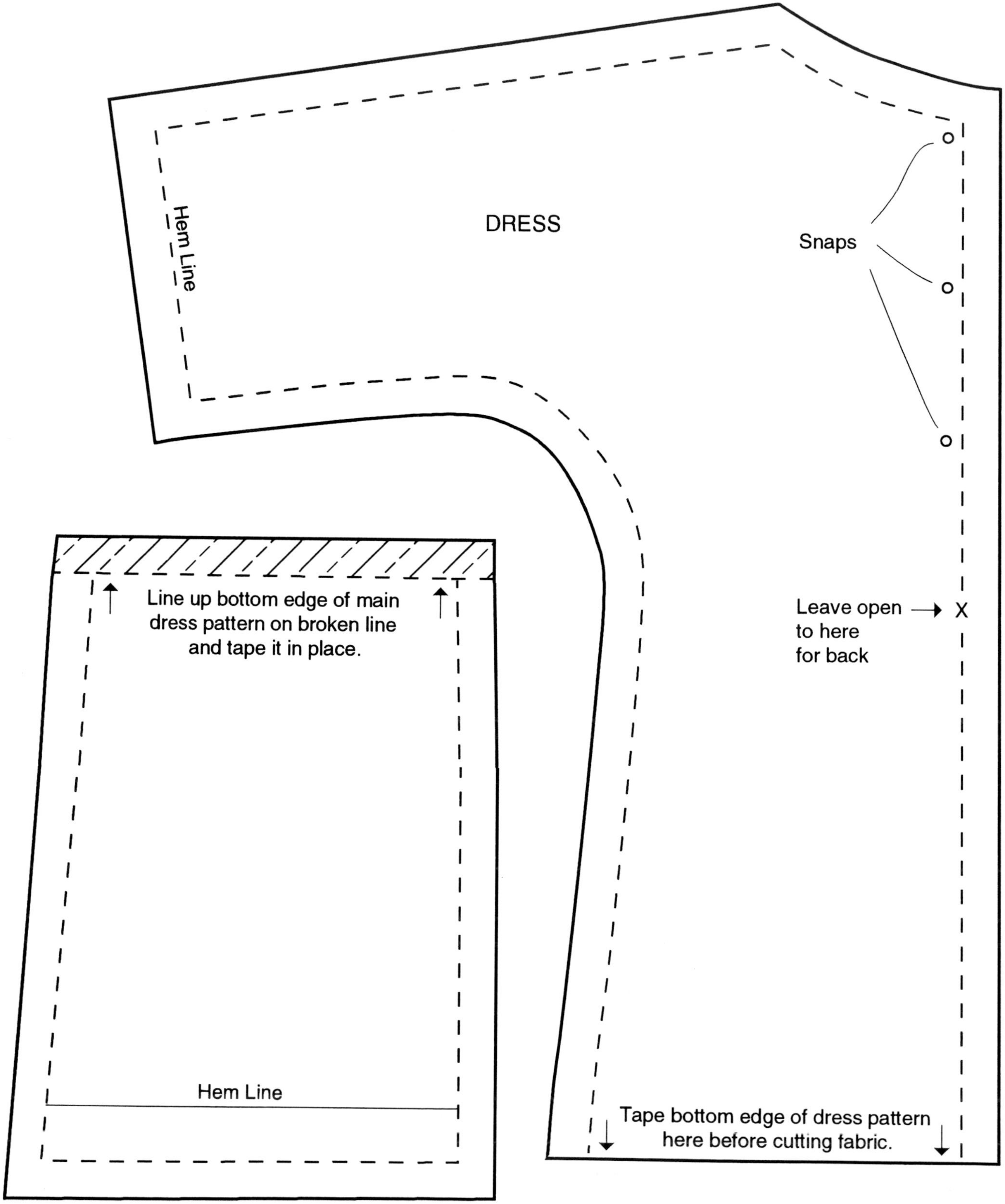

DRESS

Hem Line

Snaps

Leave open → X
to here
for back

Line up bottom edge of main
dress pattern on broken line
and tape it in place.

Hem Line

Tape bottom edge of dress pattern
here before cutting fabric.

Ties
—X—
X Side
ties

WAIST BAND / TOP TIES
(Cut 2)

Cut here →
for ties

Side X
ties

Cut 2 for waist band
Cut 2 for ties

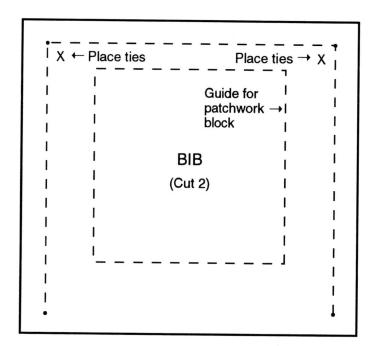

X ← Place ties   Place ties → X

Guide for
patchwork →
block

BIB

(Cut 2)

For Blocks of Patchwork and Doll Quilt:

"Lover's Knot"

Miniature "Snow Block" Chair Pincushion

Nothing lifts the spirits on a dreary winter day like a brisk cup of tea. Cozy Winter Tea Mix is a homemade blend of Earl Grey and fruit teas. To surprise a friend, tuck the tea packet inside a seat cushion sewn to fit a miniature chair. After the tea packet is removed, the cushion can be refilled with fiberfill to use as a pincushion. The patchwork pattern chosen for the matching chair back and seat cushions is a wintry traditional design called Snow Block. Each piece is 6¾" × 6¾".

SUPPLIES

miniature chair, 6"–7" across × 12" high
scraps of white, blue check, and blue pindot fabrics
1½ yards white piping
⅓ yard ½" blue satin ribbon
scrap of fiberfill batting
three ¼" snaps

CUTTING GUIDE

For each Snow Block (make 2):
1 white A
4 blue check A's
4 white B's
4 blue check C's
2 blue pindot D strips 1½" × 4¾"
2 blue pindot E strips 1½" × 6¾"
Additional pieces for cushion:
2 blue pindot backs 6¾" × 6¾"
1 fiberfill batting square 6¾" × 6¾"

DIRECTIONS

Make two Snow Block patchwork blocks following Diagram 1. For each block, sew blue check A's and blue check C's together in pairs (a). Sew white B's to sides of 2 A's (b). Sew two remaining blue check A/C pieces to sides of white A (c). Sew one of the pieced A/B/C triangles to top of A/C strip (d). Sew the second pieced triangle to the bottom to complete the block (e). Turn each block on its side (f). Frame each block by sewing 2 D strips to sides, then 2 E strips to top and bottom edges. Piece should measure 6¾" × 6¾".

Sew piping around edge of each block, butting ends for a neat finish (page 20). Place blocks and blue pindot backs together, right sides facing and edges matching. Stitch all around, securing piping in seam; leave a 2" opening on one side for turning. Clip corners and turn right side out.

To complete the chair back cushion, insert fiberfill batting into one cushion. Sew closed from back, making tiny stitches. Quilt around all white A and B blocks in outline quilting. Sew the ribbon to the center back of the cushion, following Diagram 2. Tie cushion to chair back.

To complete the chair seat cushion, separate the snaps into three male and three female pieces. Sew three male snap halves, evenly spaced, to the open inside edge of the cushion top. Sew female snaps in corresponding positions to the open inside edge of the cushion back.

TEA TIME

Tradition, Presentation, and Recipes

Lemon Grove
CAFFEINE FREE
HERB·TEA·BAG

COZY
WINTER
TEA

To make tea packet, photocopy the label, enlarging as desired (label shown in photograph was photocopied at 141 percent of original). Using colored pencils or felt-tip pens, color in trees and border. Cut out label and glue to front of zip-lock bag. Fill bag with tea leaves and seal. Slip the bag inside the seat cushion and snap closed.

Diagram 1
Snow Block Assembly

(a)

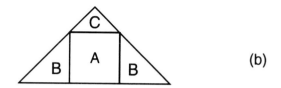

(b)

(c)

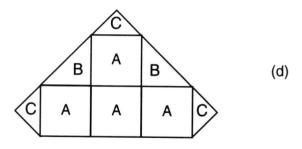

(d)

Cozy Winter Tea Mix

½ cup Earl Grey tea leaves
½ cup apricot tea leaves
½ cup raspberry tea leaves

In a bowl, mix leaves of all three teas until well blended. Spoon tea leaves into a zip-lock plastic bag with decorated label, and seal closed to keep in freshness. *Makes 24 cups of tea.*

Note: Select regular or decaffeinated tea leaves, according to the preference of the gift recipient.

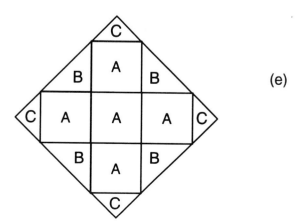

(e)

Label for Tea
Zip-Lock Bag

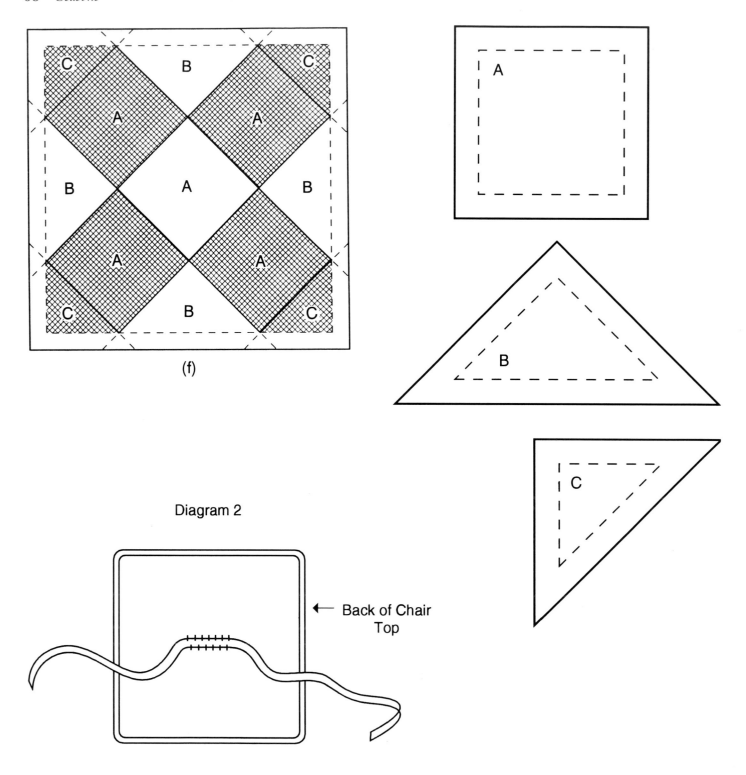

(f)

Diagram 2

← Back of Chair
Top

Sew ribbon to center back.

Special Occasions

It seems each year brings as many birthdays and other special events in
our lives as holidays! These small quilted treasures and sweet treats
make each occasion even more memorable.

Tulip Wreath Jar Topper

Friends with early spring birthdays will love to receive this patchwork tulip wreath. The two-in-one wreath tops a jar of Sweet and Spicy Walnuts for gift-giving, then moves to the wall for a lasting birthday memento. When you need a gift in a hurry, look no further than these crunchy walnut treats—they can be readied for baking in about 10 minutes. Wreath opening fits a 5"-diameter jar cover; overall wreath diameter is 6"–7", excluding the extending branches.

SUPPLIES

Note: The yellow and blue tulip covers pictured are variations of the same design. Supplies and directions below are for yellow tulip cover. They can be adapted to make the blue tulip version.

6" vine wreath
⅛ yard unbleached muslin
scraps of yellow print, green print, and pink print
    fabrics
5" piece 1⁄16" pink ribbon
scrap of fiberfill batting
glue gun

CUTTING GUIDE

2 yellow A's
4 green A's
6 muslin A's
1 yellow B
2 muslin B's
1 pink stamen C
1 green stem D
2 muslin background circles
1 fiberfill batting circle without seam allowance

DIRECTIONS

Make patchwork tulip block following Tulip Block Diagram. Sew 2 yellow A's and 4 green A's to 6 muslin A's in pairs, for 6 A/A squares. Fold two edges of stamen C and two long edges of stem D to wrong side, as indicated on patterns, and prepare for appliqué (page 18). Appliqué C to lower corner of one muslin B, matching raw edges. Appliqué D diagonally across second muslin B; trim ends even with edges of muslin. Sew a green A/A square, a yellow A/A square, and appliquéd stamen B together to make row 1. Sew a green A/A square, yellow B, and a yellow A/A square together to make row 2. Sew appliquéd stem B, and two remaining green A/A squares together to make row 3. Sew the rows together to complete the tulip block. Block should measure 3½" × 3½".

Prepare the pieced tulip block for appliqué. Position on right side of one muslin background circle and appliqué in place. Place two circles together, right sides facing and edges matching. Stitch all around, leaving an opening for turning. Clip curve all around, then turn right side out. Insert batting into opening and maneuver so it fills out the shape. Sew opening closed with tiny stitches.

Set the vine wreath face down on a flat surface. Lay muslin circle face up and apply hot glue around the edge. Set muslin circle face down into wreath opening, pressing glued edge into vines for a secure hold. Apply additional glue if necessary. Position the wreath face up with tulip appliqué on point. Tie ribbon to back of wreath at top for a hanging loop.

Sweet and Spicy Walnuts

white of 1 large egg
 1 tablespoon water
 ½ cup granulated sugar
 ½ teaspoon ground allspice
 ½ teaspoon ground cinnamon
 ½ teaspoon salt
 1 cup walnut halves

baking sheet, greased

Preheat oven to 300°F. In a small mixing bowl, beat egg white and water together at high speed until foamy but not stiff. In a separate small bowl, combine sugar, allspice, cinnamon, and salt. Drop nuts in the egg white mixture and stir until completely coated. Remove nuts from egg white mixture with a slotted spoon and stir into the sugar-spice mixture until evenly coated. Transfer coated nuts to a greased baking sheet and spread into a single layer. Toast in oven for 1 hour. Let cool on sheet, stirring occasionally to prevent sticking.
Makes about 1 cup.

Tulip Block Diagram

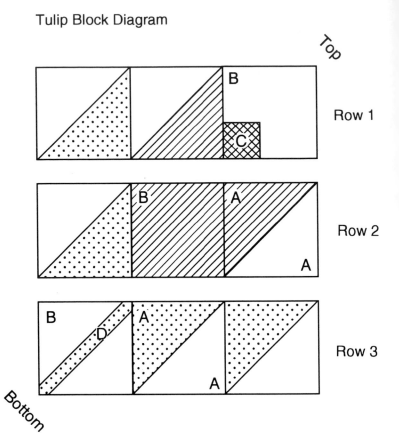

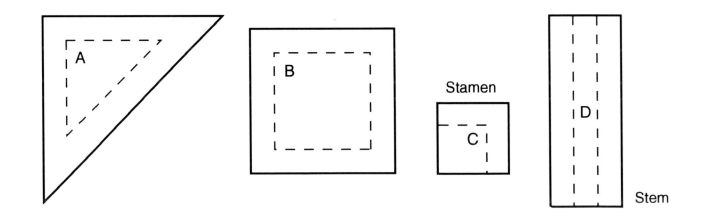

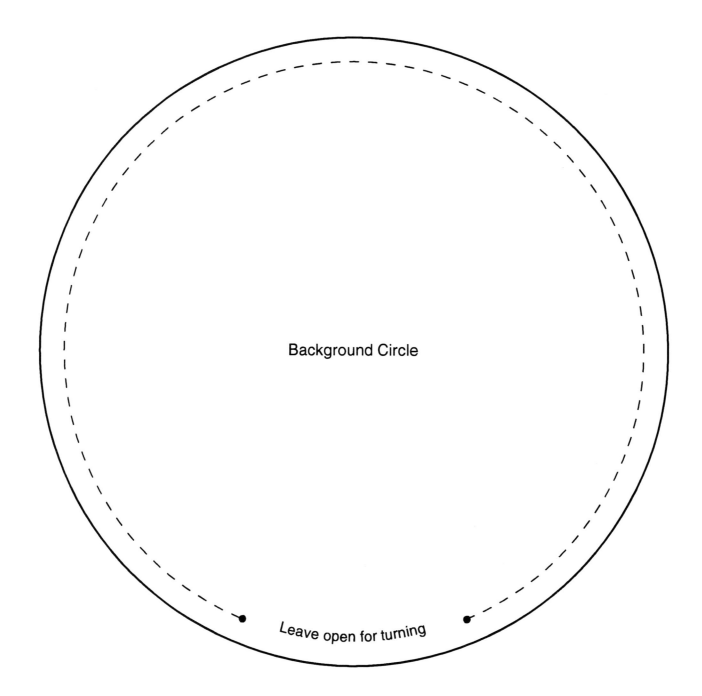

Background Circle

Leave open for turning

"Little Cedar Tree" Hat

To decorate this fun-to-wear hat, glue the deep brim up in front and add silk flowers, ribbons, and a cute patchwork block called Little Cedar Tree. Present the hat to a special friend upside-down and filled to the brim with Aunt Mollie's Oatmeal Cookies. This classic recipe comes from my old college roommate Sally Evans, who despite her busy student schedule was never too tired to bake tantalizing treats for the girls who shared our house. The Little Cedar Tree block is 4½" × 4½"; choose a hat size to fit your gift recipient.

SUPPLIES

Note: The green and peach Little Cedar Tree blocks shown in photograph are variations of the same design. Supplies and directions below are for green block. They can be adapted to make the peach version.

white woven hat with 5" crown and 3" brim
scraps of dark green print and light green plaid
    fabrics
⅝ yard light lavender single-fold bias tape
    scrap of fiberfill batting
dark purple and white silk flowers
2½ yards 1" green/purple/white print ribbon
glue gun

CUTTING GUIDE

4 light green A's
4 dark green A's
1 light green back 4½" × 4½"
1 fiberfill batting square 4½" × 4½"

DIRECTIONS

Make one Little Cedar Tree block following Diagram 1. Sew light green A's and dark green A's together in pairs to make 4 A/A squares (a). Sew squares together in pairs to make rows 1 and 2; make sure diagonal seams in each block run from lower right to upper left (b). Sew rows 1 and 2 together to make finished block measuring 4½" × 4½".

Place the pieced block and back together, wrong sides facing, and slip the batting in between. Line up the edges, then baste all around. Bind with light lavender bias binding (page 19). Quilt all light green A's in outline quilting (page 17).

To decorate the hat, fold the front brim up against the crown and hot-glue in place. Put a dab of glue on center back of quilted block and glue to center of turned-up brim. Make bow following Diagram 2. Cut two 8" and two 5" lengths of printed ribbon. Bring ends of each 8" piece together, pinch to form a point, and hot-glue to secure (a). Cut a V-shaped notch in one end of each 5" piece (b). Hot-glue pinched end of loop to short straight end (c). Hot-glue each section to hat under quilted block so "bow" extends on each side (see photograph). Glue flowers to hat around bow and block. Cut remaining ribbon in half, for two 32" lengths. Glue ends to inside crown at sides for ties. For gift-giving, turn hat upside down, set wrapped cookies inside crown, and tie hat ribbons over the top.

Aunt Mollie's Oatmeal Cookies

½ cup butter, softened at room temperature
½ cup granulated sugar
½ cup brown sugar
1 large egg, beaten
1 cup all-purpose flour
½ teaspoon salt
½ teaspoon baking powder
½ teaspoon baking soda
1 cup quick-cooking oats
½ cup shredded coconut
½ cup chopped walnuts
½ cup raisins, finely ground in food processor or
  blender
1 teaspoon vanilla extract

cookie sheets, greased

Preheat oven to 350°F. In a medium mixing bowl, cream butter until light, fluffy, and lemon-colored. Cream in sugars, then add egg and beat until smooth. Sift flour, salt, baking powder, and baking soda together and mix into butter mixture until well combined. Stir in oats, coconut, nuts, raisins, and vanilla extract with a wooden spoon. Drop by rounded tablespoonfuls 2 inches apart on a greased cookie sheet. Bake 8 to 10 minutes, or until lightly browned; do not overbake, as cookies should be chewy, not crisp. Cool on a wire rack.
Makes about 24 cookies.

Diagram 1
Block Assembly

(a)

(b) 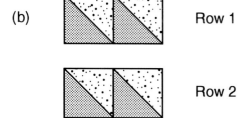 Row 1

Row 2

Top
(c)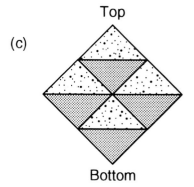
Bottom

Diagram 2
Bow

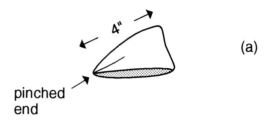

pinched
end

(a)

(b)

(c)

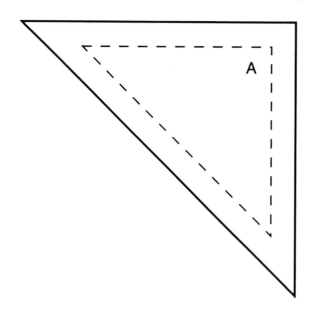

A

"Flower Pot" Keepsake Box and Pot Holder

A gift box of scrumptious Mini Cheesecakes will make an elegant addition to the bridal shower or wedding reception. When all the cakes are eaten, newlyweds can use the box to hold mementos of their wedding—a little bag of rice, the bride's garter, their invitation—for years to come. The patchwork pattern featured on the top is called Flower Pot and dates from the 1920s. A pot holder worked in the same pattern makes a welcome companion gift. Box is 7¼" × 7¼" × 4"; pot holder is 7" × 7".

SUPPLIES

white gift box 7" × 7" × 4" with 1"-deep lift-off
    cover
½ yard yellow print fabric
scraps of white, yellow, and dark blue solid or print
    fabrics
2½ yards pink piping
1½" green single-fold bias tape
1 skein each pink and dark blue embroidery floss
scrap of fiberfill batting
glue gun

KEEPSAKE BOX CUTTING GUIDE

4 white A's
4 white B's
4 yellow B's
4 dark blue B's
1 white C
2 white D's
2 dark blue D's
3 yellow print E's
1 white E (do not cut until embroidery is
    completed; see directions)
1 yellow print square 14" × 14"
1 yellow print square 7½" × 7½"
1 fiberfill batting square 5" × 5"

KEEPSAKE BOX DIRECTIONS

Make Flower Pot patchwork block rows 1–5 referring to Diagram 1. Sew 2 white A's to 1 yellow B to make rows 1 and 3 (a). Sew white, yellow, dark blue, yellow, and white B's together to make row 2 (b). Sew two dark blue B's to a white C to make row 4 (c). Appliqué light green bias tape to center of C to make flower stem (d). Sew 2 white and 2 dark blue D's together in pairs (e). Sew 2 D/D squares to dark blue B in mirror image with dark blue edges touching (f). Sew white B's to each end to complete row 5 (g). Join rows 1–5 together to complete the block. Block should measure 5½" × 5½".

Sew pink piping around the edge of block, butting ends for a neat finish (page 20). Center block on top of batting square and baste. Quilt around flower and pot in outline quilting (page 17). Fold raw edges to wrong side and press.

Transfer one E side panel outline and lettering to white fabric. Place fabric in embroidery hoop (page 17). With three strands floss in needle, embroider verse in dark blue backstitch, flower petals in pink satin stitch, and flower stamen in dark blue satin stitch. Cut out on marked lines. Sew

BLESSINGS ON THE
BRIDE AND GROOM,
MAY THEIR LOVE
FOREVER BLOOM!

pink piping around edges of embroidered white E and three yellow print E's. Fold raw edges to wrong side and press.

Place larger square of yellow print fabric wrong side up on a flat surface. Center the box cover face down on top. Apply hot glue to inside rim of cover, working one side at a time. Fold fabric to inside edges. When all four edges are glued, fold in and glue excess at corners (Diagram 2). Press edges of smaller yellow print square ¼" to wrong side twice. Glue to underside of box top, concealing all raw edges.

Glue Flower Pot block to center of box cover. Glue embroidered E panel to front of box. Glue remaining three E's to sides and back of box.

POT HOLDER SUPPLIES

¼ yard dark blue solid or print fabric
scraps of white, yellow, and pink solid or print
    fabric
⅞ yard pink piping
2" piece ¼" blue ribbon
1½" green single–fold bias tape
scrap of fiberfill batting

POT HOLDER CUTTING GUIDE

4 white A's
4 pink B's
4 yellow B's
4 white B's
1 white C
2 yellow D's
2 white D's
2 dark blue F strips ½" × 5½"
2 dark blue G strips 1½" × 7½"
1 dark blue back 7½" × 7½"
1 fiberfill batting square 7" × 7"

POT HOLDER DIRECTIONS

Make Flower Pot patchwork block rows 1–5 referring to Keepsake Box Diagram 1. Sew 2 white A's to 1 pink B to make rows 1 and 3 (a). Sew white, pink, yellow, pink, and white B's together to make row 2 (b). Sew 2 yellow B's to a white C to make row 4 (c). Appliqué light green bias tape to center of C to make flower stem (d). Sew white and yellow D's together in pairs (e). Sew 2 D/D squares to yellow B in mirror image with yellow edges touching (f). Sew white B's to each end to complete row 5 (g). Sew rows 1–5 together to complete the block. Frame the block by sewing two dark blue F strips to the top and bottom, then two dark blue G strips to the sides. Finished block should measure 7½" × 7½".

Sew pink piping around edge of block, butting ends for a neat finish (page 20). Fold blue ribbon in half and pin ends to one corner. Place finished block and back together, right sides facing and edges matching. Stitch all around, securing piping in seam; leave an opening on one side for turning. Clip corners and turn right side out. Insert batting into opening and maneuver so it fills out the shape. Sew opening closed from back, making tiny stitches. Quilt around flower and pot in outline quilting (page 17).

Mini Cheesecakes

Crust:
2 cups graham cracker crumbs
2 teaspoons granulated sugar
⅓ cup butter, melted
30 individual 1" × ¾" petits fours liner cups

baking sheet

Filling:
2 8-oz. bars cream cheese, softened at room
    temperature
¾ cup granulated sugar
3 large eggs, separated
1 teaspoon vanilla extract
2 teaspoons orange juice

Topping:
1 cup sour cream
1 tablespoon granulated sugar
1 tablespoon vanilla extract
3 graham cracker squares, crushed (optional)
1 21-oz. can cherry pie filling (optional)

Preheat oven to 350°F. In a medium-sized bowl, mix graham cracker crumbs, sugar, and melted butter together until light yellow and gritty with a firm consistency. Press about 1 tablespoon of the mixture into the bottom of each liner cup. In a medium mixing bowl, cream the cream cheese until soft and fluffy, then add the sugar and cream in well. Mix in the egg yolks, vanilla extract, and orange juice until well blended. In a small bowl, beat egg whites until stiff. Gently fold beaten egg whites into cream cheese mixture. Spoon mixture into cups about two-thirds full. Place cups on baking sheet and bake for 10 minutes. Remove from oven and let cool 2 minutes; filling will settle down a little. In a small bowl, mix sour cream, sugar, and vanilla extract until well-blended and smooth. Spoon sour cream topping over filling, and return cups to oven for another 5 minutes, or until top layer appears firm but is not yet brown. Let cool on baking sheet. Sprinkle graham cracker crumbs or spoon a small amount of cherry pie filling on top of each cake if desired.
Makes 30 mini cheesecakes.

Diagram 1

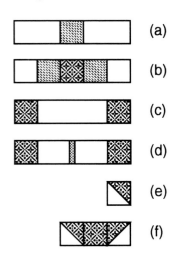

(a)
(b)
(c)
(d)
(e)
(f)
(g)

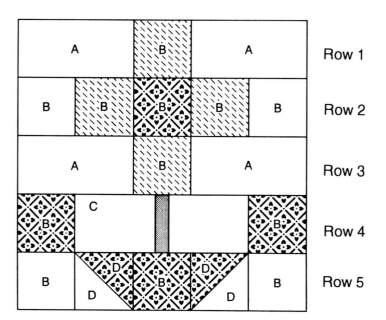

Row 1
Row 2
Row 3
Row 4
Row 5

Flower Pot Block

Diagram 2

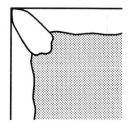

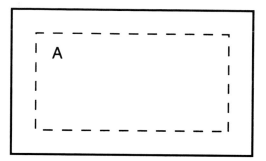

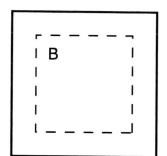

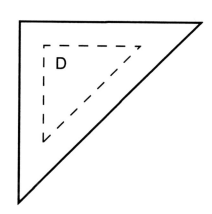

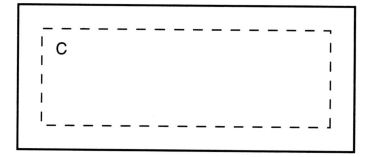

E **BLESSINGS ON THE BRIDE AND GROOM, MAY THEIR LOVE ❀FOREVER BLOOM!**

Bird's "Home Sweet Home" Nest with Blessing Tag

This pretty rose-trimmed nest is the perfect gift for a friend who is busy "feathering the nest" of a new living situation. Dried flowers are delicately intertwined with ribbon around the edge of the nest. A sweetly embroidered signpost and companion gift tag will help a friend's new surroundings seem like home right away. Inside the nest are delectable homemade Praline Eggs. You can substitute jelly beans, gum balls, or even a small purchased gift. Nest has a 4" opening; blessing tag is 1½" × 2¾".

BIRD'S NEST SUPPLIES

twig bird's nest, 6"–7" across with 4" opening
scrap of white fabric
scrap of white felt
1 yard ½" teal ribbon
1 skein each teal, green, melon, and rose embroidery floss
7 dried rose-colored roses
48 dried melon-colored star flowers
4 stems dried Queen Anne's lace
bird ornament 1"–2" long
3"–4" twig
scrap of lightweight cardboard
glue gun

BIRD'S NEST CUTTING GUIDE

1 white fabric rectangle 4¼" × 4¾" (do not cut until embroidery is completed; see directions)
1 white felt rectangle 1¾" × 2¼"
1 lightweight cardboard rectangle 2¼" × 2¾"

BIRD'S NEST DIRECTIONS

Trace cutting line, inner border, words, and flower of Home Sweet Home sign on right side of white fabric. Place fabric in embroidery hoop (page 17). Using two strands floss in needle, embroider words in teal backstitch and flower stem in green backstitch. Using three strands floss in needle, embroider leaves in green satin stitch, flower in melon satin stitch, and border in rose chain stitch. Cut out on cutting line.

Place embroidered sign face down on a flat surface. Center cardboard rectangle on top. Apply glue to edges and center of cardboard. Fold edges of sign onto cardboard, mitering corners. Glue white felt rectangle to back to conceal all raw edges. Glue twig "post" to back of sign at ×'s. Glue small bird to sign at upper right. Glue dried star flowers and Queen Anne's lace around chain-stitched border. Glue post extension to inside back wall of nest.

To decorate nest, glue two dried roses on each side of signpost. Glue remaining roses evenly spaced around top of nest. Fill spaces in between roses with sprigs of star flowers and Queen Anne's lace. Weave teal ribbon in and out around roses so ends meet in front. Tie ends in a bow. Fill in any remaining bare spaces with dried flowers.

BLESSING TAG SUPPLIES

scrap of white fabric
½ yard ⅟₁₆" rose ribbon
10" rose piping
 1 skein each teal, green, and melon embroidery
    floss

BLESSING TAG CUTTING GUIDE

2 white tags (do not cut until embroidery is
  completed; see directions)

BLESSING TAG DIRECTIONS

Trace the tag outline twice on right side of white
fabric. Trace the words, heart, and leaves inside
one tag. Place the fabric in an embroidery hoop
(page 17). Using two strands floss in needle,
embroider the words in teal backstitch, heart in
melon satin stitch, and leaves in green satin stitch.

Cut out both tags on the marked lines. Sew piping around edge of front tag, butting ends for a
neat finish (page 20). Place front and back tags
together, right sides facing. Stitch all around,
securing piping in seam; leave an opening for turning. Turn right side out. Sew closed from back,
making tiny stitches. Tie an overhand knot at midpoint of rose ribbon. Position knot on back of tag
at spot marked by O on pattern and sew in place.
Tie ribbon ends to nest.

Praline Eggs

2 cups brown sugar
1 cup heavy cream
2 tablespoons butter
2 cups pecans, finely chopped
confectioners' sugar

baking sheets lined with plastic wrap, then buttered

Combine brown sugar and cream in a saucepan. Bring
to a boil, stirring constantly until sugar dissolves and
candy thermometer reaches 238°F. Remove from heat
and add butter. Let sit a few moments until butter
melts, then add nuts and stir until well blended. Drop
by tablespoonful onto buttered plastic wrap spread
across a cookie sheet. Mold each drop into an egg
shape with your fingers and position eggs 1 inch apart.
Let cool, then roll in confectioners' sugar.
Makes about 30 eggs.

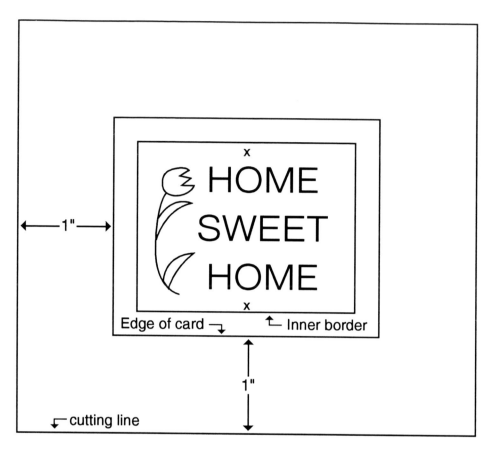

HOME
SWEET
HOME

x

x

Edge of card ↳   ↰ Inner border

1"

1"

↳ cutting line

Home Sweet Home Sign
Sign Size: 2 1/4" x 2 3/4"

x = Glue twig to back

MAY YOUR
NEW NEST
BE BLESSED

Sew ribbon to O →

Leave open
for turning

House and Heart Tray

Create this house and heart appliqué design for the family that is moving to a new home. They'll welcome a trayful of Janet's Chewies to munch on while they're unpacking, and they'll delight to discover the heartwarming house motif that appears on the tray as the bars disappear. Linda Currie contributed this original recipe, which her mom Janet DeFilipio created for her family over forty years ago. Appliqué panel fits a 9" × 15" tray.

SUPPLIES

Note: Tray shown has a 9" × 15" design area. Project patterns can be adapted for a slightly larger tray if desired.

wooden tray with glass top designed to accept 9" × 15" inset; tray kit should include precut 9" × 15" cardboard backing
⅓ yard cream print fabric
scraps of light lavender print, medium lavender print, dark lavender print, and medium green print fabric
1 skein each light lavender, dark lavender, and green embroidery floss
fiberfill batting
masking tape

CUTTING GUIDE

1 cream print rectangle 11" × 17", or 2" larger than tray opening all around (do not cut until embroidery is completed; see directions)
1 medium green A
1 light lavender B
1 medium lavender C
4 dark lavender D's
1 fiberfill batting rectangle 9" × 15"

DIRECTIONS

Using a photocopy machine, enlarge the Placement Diagram to 127 percent of the original. Measure and mark an 11" × 17" rectangle on right side of cream print fabric. Trace the enlarged heart, house, and vine designs, centered, inside the marked area. Place fabric in an embroidery hoop (page 17). Using three strands floss in needle, embroider leaves in green satin stitch, vines in green chain stitch, and berries in light and medium lavender satin stitch. Remove fabric from hoop and cut out rectangle on marked line.

Prepare house pieces A, B, and C and four D hearts for appliqué (page 18), clipping into corners as indicated on patterns. Appliqué each house piece in its position on cream background block. Appliqué a heart in each corner.

Lay the appliquéd piece face down on a flat surface. Center the batting and cardboard on top. Fold fabric edges tautly over cardboard edges and tape securely. Install assembled piece in tray under glass, following tray manufacturer's directions.

Janet's Chewies

  2 cups semisweet chocolate chips
22 graham cracker squares, crushed (about 2 cups)
  1 14-oz. can sweetened condensed milk
 ¾ cup pecans, chopped

8" square baking pan (do not use glass), heavily
   greased and lightly floured

Preheat oven to 350°F. Mix all ingredients together in a bowl until completely blended and firm. Pour mixture into greased and floured pan. Bake for 35 minutes, or until top is lightly browned. Let cool in pan for 10 minutes, then turn upside down onto a cutting board and lift off pan. Cut into 2-inch squares with a sharp knife.
Makes 16 squares.

Note: To vary the recipe, substitute 1 cup white chocolate chips or 1 cup peanut butter chips for 1 cup semisweet chocolate chips.

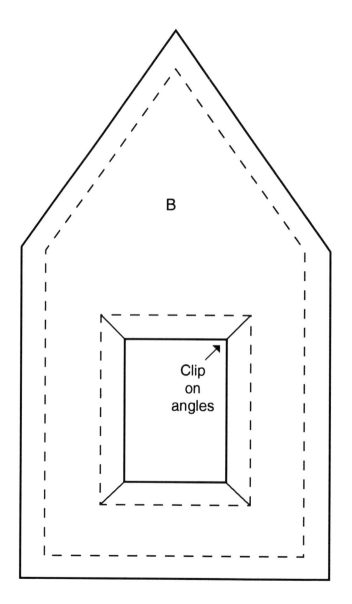

B

Clip
on
angles

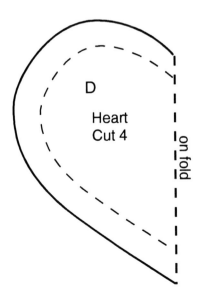

D

Heart
Cut 4

on fold

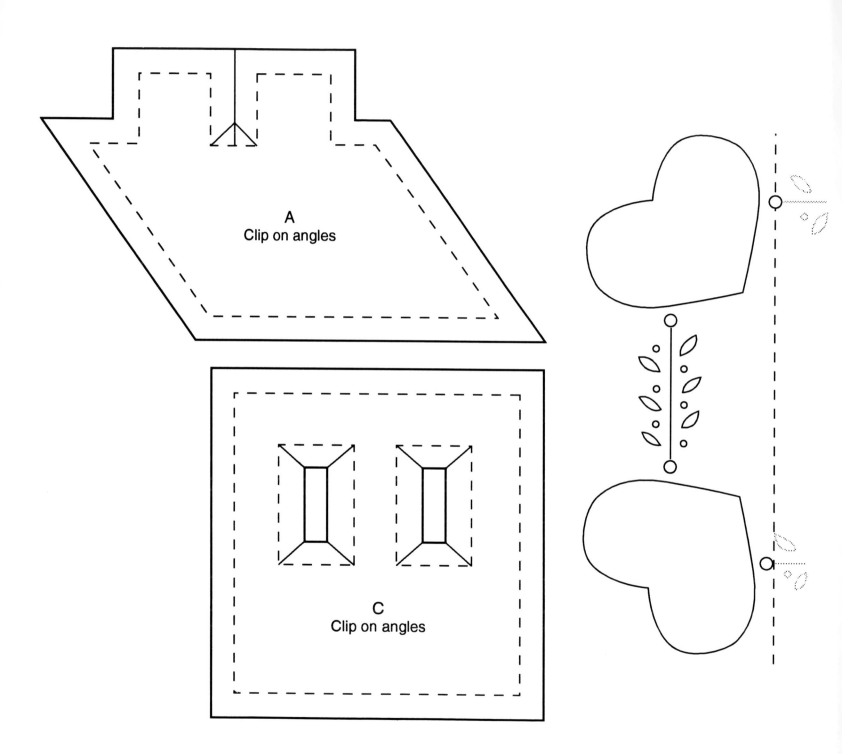

A
Clip on angles

C
Clip on angles

Placement Diagram
Enlarge 127%

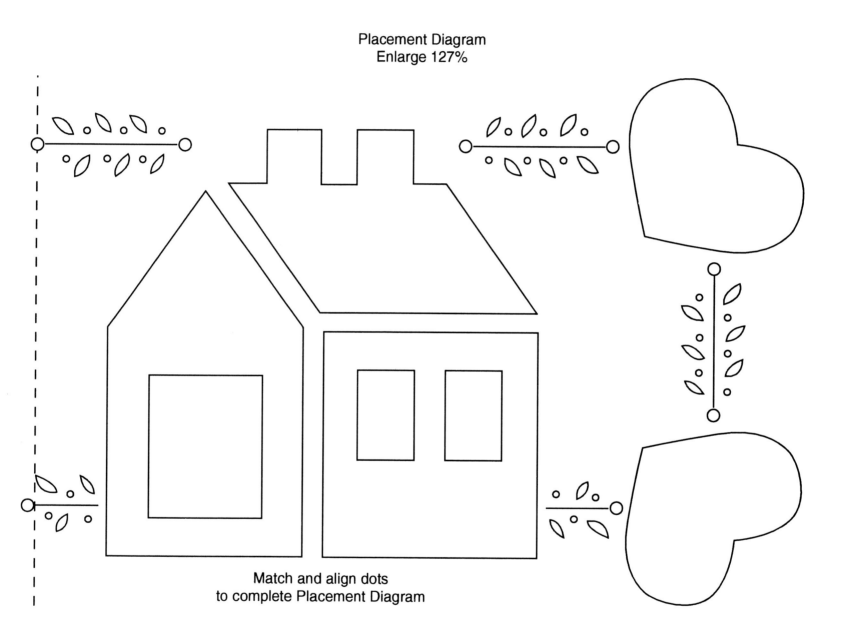

Match and align dots
to complete Placement Diagram

Birdcage with Lovebird Tag

An inexpensive wicker birdcage I found at an import store inspired this romantic gift. Dried roses, leaves, and other flowers decorate the outside, and a removable heart garland is draped across the door. The embroidered lovebird tag adds a note of whimsy. Since the floor of the cage is removable, I found it very easy to insert an ample supply of Heart Shortbread Cookies. Birdcage is 8" × 12"; tag is 2¾" × 1¼".

BIRDCAGE SUPPLIES

wicker birdcage 8" across × 12" high
gold, silver, or white nontoxic spray paint
18 dried dark pink roses
 4 light pink dried larkspurs
 9 dried leaves
scraps of gold lamé, light pink, and dark rose fabric
⅝ yard ⅟₁₆" light pink satin ribbon
⅝ yard ⅟₁₆" dark rose satin ribbon
⅜ yard ½" pink satin ribbon
fiberfill
glue gun

BIRDCAGE CUTTING GUIDE

2 gold lamé hearts
4 pink hearts
4 rose hearts

DIRECTIONS

Spray the birdcage and base with gold, silver, or white paint, as desired, following paint manufacturer's directions. Let dry, then spray a second coat. Let dry completely.

Tie the ½" pink satin ribbon in a bow around the hanger at top of cage. Using a glue gun, attach a cluster of roses and pink larkspur to the bow knot. Trim ribbon ends diagonally, then glue streamers to cage bars. Glue roses, pink larkspur, and leaves in a ring around top crossbar of the cage, alternating colors. Glue extra flowers and leaves above.

Place the 10 fabric hearts together in pairs, right sides facing; stitch all around, leaving an opening for turning. Clip curves, bottom point, and top center; turn right side out. Stuff lightly with fiberfill. Sew openings closed, making tiny stitches. Quilt around each heart ¼" from edge. You should have 1 gold lamé heart, 2 pink hearts, and 2 rose hearts.

Arrange hearts in a row following Garland Diagram. Place pink hearts (#2) edge to edge with gold heart (#1), then slip pink edges behind gold edges. Place rose hearts (#3) on each end, with edges slipped under pink heart edges. Sew together by hand from the back. Cut each ⅟₁₆" ribbon in half, for pieces approximately 11" long. Hold light and dark pieces together in pairs, and make an overhand knot at the midpoint. Sew each knot to the back outer edge of a #3 rose heart, marked by × on pattern. Attach garland to birdcage by tying ribbon streamers to crossbars, centering so gold heart is above door.

LOVEBIRD TAG SUPPLIES

scrap of white fabric
⅓ yard pink piping
6" piece ¹⁄₁₆" light pink satin ribbon
1 skein each pink, blue, and peach embroidery
   floss

LOVEBIRD TAG CUTTING GUIDE

2 white tags (do not cut until embroidery is
   completed; see directions)

LOVEBIRD TAG DIRECTIONS

Trace the tag outline twice on right side of white
fabric. Trace the words, bird, and hearts inside one
tag. Place the fabric in an embroidery hoop (page
17). Using three strands floss in needle, embroider
the words in pink backstitch, the colon in pink
French knots, and the hearts in pink satin stitch.
Using two strands floss in needle, embroider the
bird in blue backstitch and the bird's feet and beak
in peach backstitch.

   Cut out both tags on the marked lines. Sew piping around edge of front tag, butting ends for a
neat finish (page 20). Place front and back tags
together, right sides facing and edges matching.
Stitch all around, securing piping in seam; leave an
opening for turning. Clip corners and turn right
side out. Sew closed from back, making tiny
stitches. Tie an overhand knot at midpoint of rose
ribbon. Position knot on back of tag at spot
marked by × on pattern and sew in place. Tie tag
to spoke of birdcage.

Heart Shortbread Cookies

2 cups (4 sticks) sweet unsalted butter, softened
   at room temperture
1 cup confectioners' sugar
4 cups sifted all-purpose flour
16-oz. jar strawberry, cherry, or raspberry preserves

cookie sheets, greased

Preheat oven to 375°F. In a large mixing bowl, cream
the butter until light and fluffy. Add the confectioners'
sugar gradually, creaming it into butter until well blended and firm. Add the flour gradually, mixing in with a
wooden spoon until well blended. Form dough into a
ball and chill, covered, in refrigerator for ½ hour. Turn
the chilled dough onto a board lightly dusted with flour
and confectioners' sugar. Pat out dough to a ¼-inch
thickness. Place heart template on top of dough and
cut around it with a sharp knife dusted with flour to
make cookies. Make a small dent with your thumb in
center of each cookie and fill with preserves. Using a
toothpick, pierce tiny dots around edge of each cookie
as shown in photograph. Transfer cookies with a metal
spatula to a greased cookie sheet, setting them about 1
inch apart. Bake at 375°F for 5 minutes, then turn
oven down to 300°F and bake an additional 10 minutes, or until edges are lightly browned. Cool on a
wire rack.

Makes about 36 cookies.

Note: Cut heart template before you begin. Photocopy or trace the Shortbread Heart outline, then tape
the copy to lightweight cardboard. Cut on the marked
lines to make template.

Garland Diagram

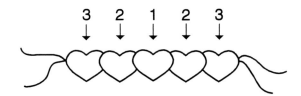

Heart Stringer
Note overlaps:
Heart 2's are under edge of 1.
Heart 3's are under edge of 2's.

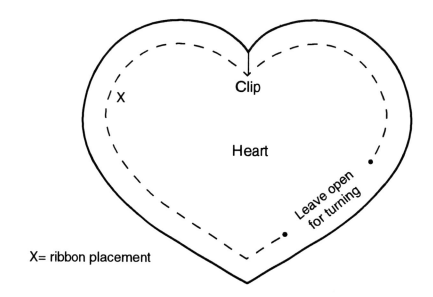

X= ribbon placement

x = Sew ribbon to back

Baby Bonnet Jar Topper

A mini basket pattern and delicate quilting are sure to charm the mother-to-be. This baby bonnet will make a welcome addition to the new baby's wardrobe, but in the meantime it tops a jar of pink or blue Pretzel Cookies for the expectant mom and dad to share. Bonnet fits sizes 6 months to 1 year.

SUPPLIES

¼ yard light blue print fabric
⅛ yard pink print fabric
scraps of pink print, blue print, and white fabrics
½ yard 1½" white pregathered eyelet trim
⅔ yard white double-fold bias tape
5" blue single-fold bias tape
scrap of fiberfill batting

CUTTING GUIDE

For each basket block (make 2):
4 white A's
4 light blue print A's
4 white B's
1 pink print B
Additional pieces for baby bonnet:
4 light blue print C's
2 light blue print D's
1 light blue print E
2 light blue print F's
1 pink print lining 5" × 16½"
1 fiberfill batting rectangle 4½" × 15"

DIRECTIONS

Make two patchwork basket blocks following Diagram 1. For each block, sew white A's and light blue print A's together in pairs to make 4 A/A squares (a). Sew white B's to 2 A/A squares to make rows 1 and 3; position so diagonal seam runs from lower right to upper left. Sew two remaining A/A squares to pink print B to make row 2 (b). Sew the rows together so pink block is in the center.

To make basket handle, cut a 2½" length of blue bias tape. Unfold the tape and trim off one edge by cutting along the foldline. Press remaining tape flat, then press both edges in so they meet in the center. Tape width should be about ¼". Press the short raw edges to wrong side. Pin handle to basket block so it arcs through white portion of block and ends touch top of basket. Appliqué in place (c).

Assemble bonnet sides and crown referring to Diagram 2. Place basket patchwork blocks on a flat surface, right side up. Turn one block so basket handle is in upper left corner. Turn other block so basket handle is in upper right corner. Pin blue print C's to block sides, right sides facing, and sew seams. Sew blue print D's to block bottoms. Sew tops of blocks to short ends of blue print E. Finished patchwork should measure 5" × 16½". Fold shorter raw edges ¼" to wrong side and steam-press.

Quilt bonnet following Diagram 3. Lay patchwork on top of batting, right side up, and baste with long, loose stitches. Quilt all white areas around basket, handle, and edge of block in outline quilting. Using quilter's tape, mark C, D, and E blocks as shown and quilt straight lines. Remove all basting threads.

Place two blue print F's together, right sides facing. Sew bottom edges together, clip curve, and fold right side out. Pin long back edge of quilted bonnet to curved raw edge of F, right sides facing. Stitch all around, easing F to fit.

Cut eyelet trim equal to long front edge of quilted bonnet plus 1". Fold ends of trim ¼" to wrong side twice and hem with tiny stitches. Pin eyelet to front edge of bonnet, right sides facing and straight edges matching; baste in place. Machine-stitch ¼" from edge. Press raw edge to wrong side along stitching line so eyelet faces forward. Press raw edges of pink lining ¼" to wrong side. Pin lining to inside of bonnet, matching folds. Stitch all around with tiny stitches, concealing raw edges and machine stitching.

To make ties, machine-stitch down a 24" length of double-fold bias binding to secure the fold. Cut in half, for two 12" pieces. Turn under raw edge at hand and hand-sew to inside corner of bonnet. Knot free ends to prevent raveling.

Pretzel Cookies

½ cup margarine, softened at room temperature
1 4-oz. bar light cream cheese
¾ cup granulated sugar
yolk of 1 large egg
1½ teaspoons almond extract
6 drops red or 6 drops blue food coloring
¼ teaspoon salt
2¼ cups presifted all-purpose flour
1 16-oz. can vanilla frosting
1 2-oz. container multicolored sugar sprinkles

cookie sheets, greased

Preheat oven to 350°F. In a large mixing bowl, cream the margarine, cream cheese, and sugar together until pale yellow and smooth. Add the egg yolk, almond extract, food coloring, and salt, and mix until smooth. Add the flour gradually, mixing in with a wooden spoon until well blended. Divide dough into four equal sections, then divide each section into eight pieces. Roll each piece out on a lightly floured board to make a 12-inch rope. Twist rope ends together once, then part the ends slightly and press them down onto the larger dough loop. Using a spatula, transfer each pretzel cookie onto cookie sheet, placing them about 1 inch apart. Bake for 10 minutes, or until lightly browned. Transfer to wire racks and let cool. Spread frosting across top of each cookie and top with sugar sprinkles.
Makes about 32 pretzel cookies.

Diagram 1

(a)

(b)
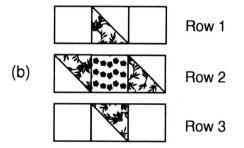

Row 1

Row 2

Row 3

(c)
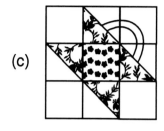

Bonnet Assembly
Piece each side like this:

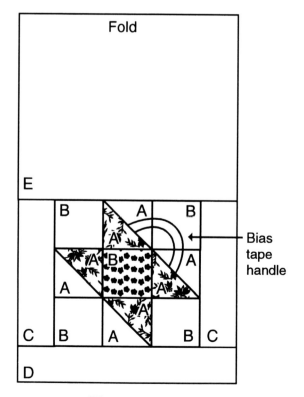

Fold

E

B

A

B

A'

A

B

A

A

A'

C

B

A

B

C

D

Bias
tape
handle

Diagram 2

Quilting Diagram
Quilt each side like this:

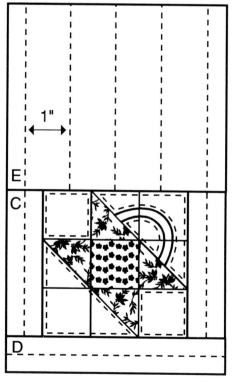

1"

E

C

D

Diagram 3

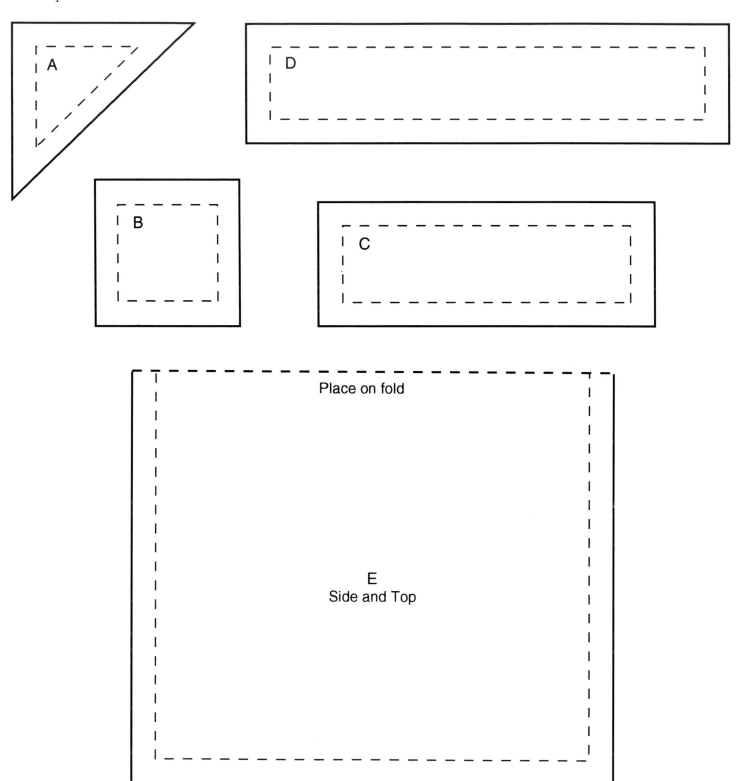

Place on fold

E
Side and Top

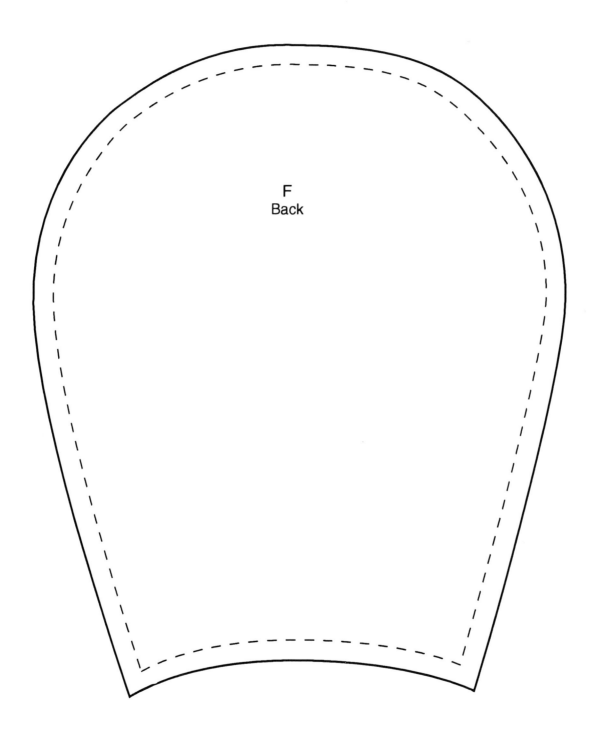

F
Back

Miniature Star Quilt

Many styles of miniature beds are sold today—I like to make pint-sized quilts for them and use them to decorate my home. To welcome a new baby, I chose a bent twig bed on rockers. I placed my Aunt Esther's Caramel Rolls (it took me thirty years to get the recipe!) on the bed and laid a sweet quilt on top. In future years, the baby-turned-little-girl can use the bed and quilt for a doll, or it can become an heirloom decoration in the family home. Quilt is 12" × 13", excluding trim.

SUPPLIES

⅜ yard pink fabric
¼ yard white/pink print fabric
scraps of medium pink print, dark pink print, and
    white/pink print fabrics
1⅛ yard 2½" white eyelet trim
fiberfill batting

CUTTING GUIDE

For star block (make 5):
8 medium pink print A's
8 white/pink print A's
4 white/pink print B's
1 medium pink print C
4 white/pink print D's
Additional pieces for quilt:
1 dark pink print E strip 1" × 12½"
1 pink back 12½" × 13"
1 fiberfill batting rectangle 12" × 12¼"

DIRECTIONS

Make five miniature star blocks following Diagram 1. For each block, sew medium pink print A's and white/pink print A's together in pairs for 8 A/A squares (a). Sew A/A squares together in pairs, matching white/pink print edges, for 4 pieced A rectangles (b). Sew white/pink print B's to ends of two pieced A rectangles to make 2 A/B strips (c). Sew two remaining rectangles to side edges of medium pink print C, so medium pink prints are touching (d). Arrange A/B strips at top and bottom of A/C strip (e). Join the three rows to complete the star block.

Assemble quilt top following Diagram 2. Join 2 star blocks to sides of white/pink print D for rows 1 and 3. Join 2 D's to sides of remaining star block for row 2. Join rows together. Sew dark pink print E strip to top of row 1 for top band. Finished quilt top should measure 12½" × 13".

Pin eyelet trim to quilt top sides and bottom, right sides facing and edges matching; sew through both layers around three edges of quilt, leaving top banded edge untrimmed. Place the quilt top and quilt back together, right sides facing and edges matching. Sew the top edges only.

Fold the quilt right side out. Slip the fiberfill in between the quilt top and back and baste with long, loose stitches. Quilt each white/pink A and B in outline quilting to make stars pop out. Using quilter's tape or a marking pen, mark diagonal lines from corner to corner in each D block and quilt an × shape. Remove basting threads.

To finish quilt, turn raw edges of back ¼" to wrong side. Pin to edge of quilt top, concealing machine stitching, and sew with small overcast stitches all around.

Aunt Esther's Caramel Rolls

½ cup warm water
2 ¼-oz. packages yeast
¼ cup granulated sugar
¼ cup shortening
2 teaspoons salt
1½ cups milk, scalded then cooled to room
   temperature
2 large eggs
7 to 7½ cups sifted all-purpose flour
6 tablespoons butter, softened at room
   temperature
1½ cups granulated sugar
1½ teaspoons ground cinnamon

two 13" x 9" x 2" pans

Pan Caramelizing:

½ cup (1 stick) butter, softened at room
   temperature
2 cups brown sugar
1 cup heavy cream

Preheat oven to 375°F. Place warm water in a very large mixing bowl, add yeast, and stir to dissolve. Add *1 teaspoon only* of the sugar, stir to dissolve, then let stand for 10 minutes. In a medium bowl, combine remaining sugar, shortening, and salt and beat briskly with a wooden spoon until well creamed. Mix in cooled milk and eggs, then transfer to the yeast bowl. Stir in half of the flour with a wooden spoon, then mix with an electric mixer set to medium for 2 minutes. Add the remaining flour, mixing by hand until the dough handles easily and pulls away from the side of the bowl. Turn onto a lightly floured board and knead for 5 minutes. Place dough in a greased bowl, greased side up, and cover with a cloth. Let rise in a warm place until doubled, about 1½ hours. Punch dough down and let rest for 15 minutes. Turn out dough and roll on a floured board. Divide dough into 3 pieces. Roll each piece into a 9" × 15" oblong. Turn out dough and roll on floured board. Spread *each* oblong with 2 tablespoons softened butter. Mix 1½ cups sugar with cinnamon until well blended, then divide in thirds, and sprinkle over top of each oblong. Roll each oblong lengthwise to make three 15-inch-long rolls. Cut each roll into fifteen 1-inch pieces. Let rolls double in size.

To prepare pans for baking, spread ¼ cup softened butter over bottom of each pan, sprinkle 1 cup brown sugar over butter, then pour ½ cup heavy cream over all. Set pans in preheated oven until sugar melts, about 5 minutes. Allow mixture to cool in pans, then set rolls in pans upright. Bake for 20 minutes, or until golden brown.
Makes 45 rolls.

Diagram 1

Diagram 2

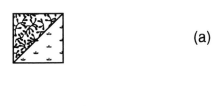

(a)

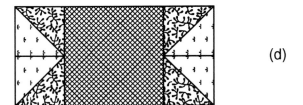

(b)

(c)

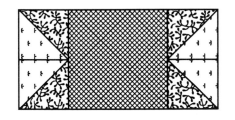

(d)

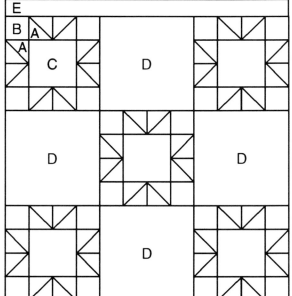

top band

Row 1

Row 2

Row 3

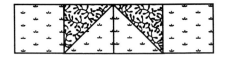

Row 1

Row 2

(e)

Row 3

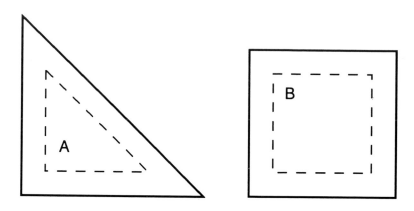

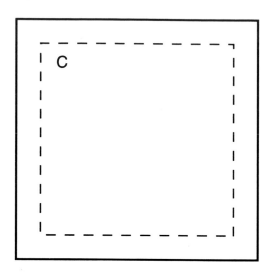

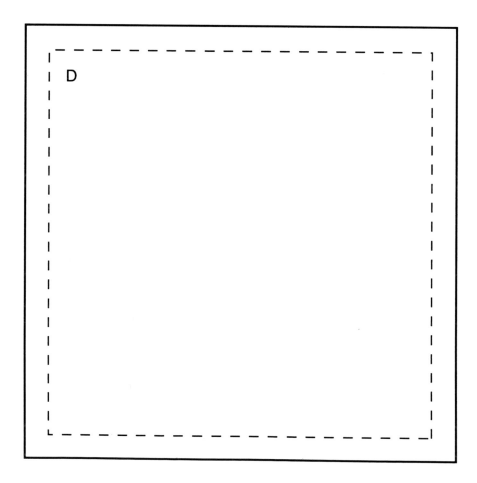

Holidays

❧

Holidays "take the cake" in gift-giving occasions! Here is a host of wonderful fabric gifts to craft and sumptuous recipes to make for friends and family, from Valentine's Day to Christmas.

"Be Mine" Candy Box

Any Valentine would love to receive this thoughtful keepsake box on the day when love is in the air. A romantic doily, gold ribbon, and embroidered heart adorn outside. Inside, your Valentine will find tempting pieces of Crunchy Vanilla Fudge—a rich homemade treat loaded with chopped almonds. Should you find the package too irresistible, the ribbon discreetly pops on and off with Velcro® fasteners. Box is 4½" across × 2½" high.

SUPPLIES

round lightweight wooden box with cover,
    4½" across × 2¼" high
red nontoxic spray paint
scrap of red pindot fabric
3½" round white crocheted doily
 ¾ yard ½" gold metallic ribbon
  1 skein white embroidery floss
½" Velcro® dot
glue gun

CUTTING GUIDE

2 red pindot hearts (do not cut until embroidery is
  completed; see directions)

DIRECTIONS

Spray the box and its cover with red paint, following paint manufacturer's directions. Let dry, then spray a second coat. Let dry completely.

Trace the heart outline twice on right side of red pindot fabric. Trace the words inside one heart. Place the fabric in an embroidery hoop (page 17). Using three strands white floss in needle, embroider the words in backstitch. Cut out both hearts on the marked lines. Place front and back hearts together, right sides facing. Stitch all around, leaving an opening for turning. Clip curves, bottom point, and top center; turn right side out. Sew opening closed with tiny stitches.

Make gold metallic bow following Bow Diagram. Cut two 4½" lengths of gold ribbon. Fold each piece in half (a), then clip ends diagonally (b). Crisscross ribbons, then glue to back of heart so points face down (c). Wrap remaining ribbon around box. Overlap ends ½" at top of box, and trim off excess; ribbon should be about 15" long. Hold ends together so ribbon forms a circle and ends overlap ½". Slip a Velcro® dot (do not separate) in between the ends and glue in place. When glue is dry, separate the dots. Glue one end to back of heart at ribbon crossover so Velcro® dot half is on top (d).

Glue doily to box cover. Fill box with fudge, then replace. Fasten gold ribbon around outside so heart is on top.

Crunchy Vanilla Fudge

2 cups granulated sugar
¼ cup sweet unsalted butter, softened at room
   temperature
⅔ cup evaporated milk
⅔ cup whole milk
¼ teaspoon almond extract
1 cup slivered almonds, finely chopped
candy red-hots (optional)

8" square baking dish, greased

Heat sugar, butter, and milks in a heavy saucepan, stirring until sugar is dissolved and butter is melted. Bring mixture to a boil and cover. Let boil for three minutes. Uncover and continue boiling until mixture reaches 240°F on candy thermometer, then remove from heat. Add almond extract and nuts and beat until mixture becomes thick and light. Pour into greased pan and spread evenly to pan edges. When mixture begins to set, use a greased knife to score top lightly into 1-inch squares. Let cool completely, then cut into squares as scored. For a Valentine's Day touch, press a candy red-hot into the top of each square just before serving (candy may run if allowed to set in fudge).
Makes about 64 candies.

Bow Diagram

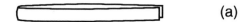 (a)

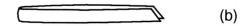 (b)

 (c)

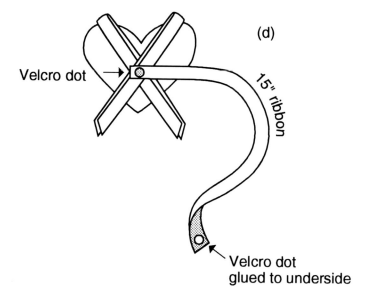

(d)

Velcro dot

15" ribbon

Velcro dot
glued to underside

clip

BE MINE

Leave open
for turning

"Sweets for the Sweet" Basket Cover

What Valentine wouldn't be charmed by ribbon roses, baby's breath, and a sweet sentiment from Shakespeare's *Hamlet*? Tucked beneath the dainty embroidered Battenburg lace doily are luscious Cherry Chocolate Cookies. Made without butter, these scrumptious cookies are low in fat—weight-watching Valentines will love you forever! Basket is 6" across × 3" deep; doily is 7" across.

SUPPLIES

basket 6" across × 3" high, excluding handle
red nontoxic spray paint
6"-7" diameter white cotton doily with Battenburg
    lace trim (trim should slightly overlap edge of
    basket)
 1 yard ½" red ribbon
 1 skein red embroidery floss
10 red ribbon flowers, each about ½" across
10 sprigs baby's breath
florist's tape

DIRECTIONS

Spray the basket with red paint, following paint manufacturer's directions. Let dry, then spray a second coat. Let dry completely.

Trace the words, hearts, and dot, centered, on the right side of the doily. Place the doily in a small embroidery hoop (page 17). Using three strands red floss in needle, embroider the words in backstitch, the hearts in satin stitch, and the dot in a French knot. Remove doily from hoop and press out wrinkles.

Arrange ribbon roses into two miniature bouquets of five roses each. Add baby's breath, then bind stems together with florist's tape. Cut ribbon in half, for two 18" lengths. Thread each ribbon through a design hole in Battenburg lace edging at opposite sides of doily. Set wrapped cookies inside basket, then set doily on top. Tie ribbons to basket handles, making a bow at each side. Slip the stem of each miniature bouquet into bow knots at opposite sides.

Cherry Chocolate Cookies

2 large egg whites
¾ cup granulated sugar
1½ teaspoons cherry extract
3 tablespoons unsweetened cocoa powder
¾ cup semisweet chocolate chips
½ cup Maraschino cherries, finely chopped
10 to 12 Maraschino cherries, halved

cookie sheets lined with greased aluminum foil

Preheat oven to 250°F. In a small mixing bowl, beat egg whites until stiff. Beat in sugar a little at a time until mixture turns shiny. Beat in cherry extract. Switch to low setting and mix in cocoa powder. Fold in chocolate chips and chopped cherries by hand, using a wooden spoon or rubber spatula. Drop by heaping teaspoonfuls 1 inch apart on a greased cookie sheet. Place a half cherry, rounded side up, in middle of each cookie; do not push down, or cherry will sink inside cookie during baking. Bake for 1 hour, or until cookies have a shiny surface. Cool on wire racks.
Makes about 20 cookies.

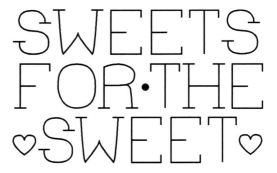

SWEETS FOR·THE ♡SWEET♡

Cherry Tart Pan Cover

George Washington's legendary confession about chopping down the cherry tree inspired me to create this patriotic tart cover. An elastic band holds the cover securely around a Cherry Crumble Tart in its baking pan. Later, the tart pan and cover can be reused to store small items such as pins or buttons. Cover fits a round 4¼" × 1" pie plate.

SUPPLIES

scraps of white/red pindot, green print, and red
    fabrics
¾ yard 2" white eyelet trim
½ yard ½" red satin ribbon
1 skein each red, green, and navy blue embroidery
    floss
⅜ yard ⅛" elastic
compass

CUTTING GUIDE

1 white/red pindot 9"circle (do not cut until
    embroidery and appliqué are completed; see
    directions)
2 green print leaves
2 red cherries

DIRECTIONS

Using a compass, mark 9" and 5" concentric circles on right side of white/red pindot fabric. Trace the tart cover pattern inside the 5" circle. Place the fabric in an embroidery hoop. Using three strands floss in needle, embroider the wavy bars in navy blue satin stitch, the stars in red satin stitch, and the cherry stems in green chain stitch. Prepare the fabric leaves and cherries for appliqué (page 18). Place each piece in position on the white/red pindot background and appliqué in place.

Cut out the 9" circle on the marked line. Press the edge ¼" to the wrong side. Machine-baste along fold. Pulling up bobbin thread slightly to create ease, fold ½" to wrong side again, and press. Machine-stitch along first fold to create casing; leave a ⅝" opening to insert elastic.

Place cover right side up. Slip eyelet trim under edge and pin all around; fold and overlap the ends, trimming off excess, for a neat finish. Topstitch close to fold. Thread elastic through casing. Test-fit on pie plate, cut elastic shorter if necessary, and sew ends together. Sew casing opening closed with tiny stitches. Place cover over plastic-wrapped tart. Wrap red ribbon around pan and tie in a bow.

Cherry Crumble Tart

Filling:

2   16-oz. cans tart pitted cherries (do not use Bing cherries)
¾ cup granulated sugar
⅓ cup cornstarch
⅛ teaspoon salt

five 4¼" × 1" pie plates
baking sheet

Crumble Topping:

¾ cup all-purpose flour
½ cup granulated sugar
½ cup rolled oats (not quick-cooking)
½ cup chopped walnuts
½ cup margarine, chilled

Preheat oven to 375°F. Drain the cherries, saving the juice. In a saucepan, stir 1 cup of the reserved cherry juice, ¼ cup of the sugar, cornstarch, and salt over a low heat until sugar is dissolved. Slowly add the rest of the juice, cooking over a medium heat and stirring constantly until mixture starts to bubble. Remove from heat, add cherries and remaining sugar, and stir until sugar is completely dissolved. Set tart pans on a baking sheet, and ladle cherry mixture into them. In a medium bowl, mix flour, sugar, rolled oats, nuts, and margarine together with your fingers until crumbly. Spoon crumble topping onto tarts. Bake for 35 to 40 minutes, or until tops are bubbly and edges are brown.
Makes 5 tarts.

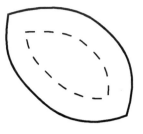

Leaf

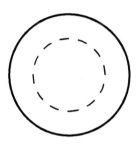

Cherry

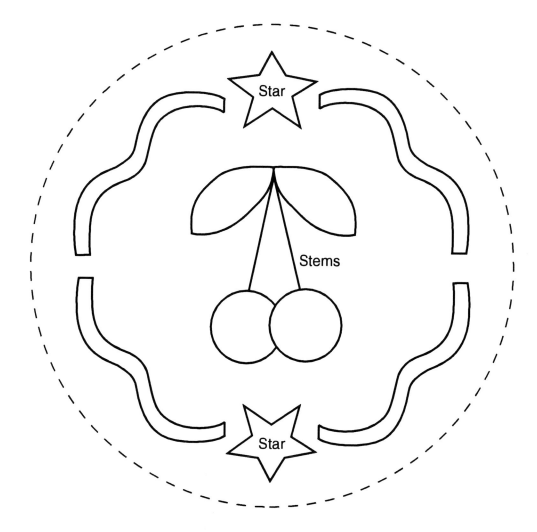

Star

Stems

Star

Tart Cover

Heather Friendship Tag and Shamrock Pins

My grandparents were born in County Fermanagh, Ireland, and my mother lived in Ireland during her childhood. Every year when St. Patrick's day rolls around, I enjoy celebrating this side of my heritage. Currant Soda Bread, a classic rich bread from the Emerald Isle, makes a handsome gift when set on a plate and wrapped in cellophane. I've added a friendship tag embroidered with a warm Irish saying and two fabric shamrocks that can be pinned to clothing or a tote bag. Friendship tag is 4" × 4"; shamrock pins are 3½" × 3¼".

HEATHER FRIENDSHIP TAG SUPPLIES

scrap of white/light green print fabric
⅝ yard ¼" orange satin ribbon
⅝ yard ¼" decorative white trim
1 skein each light green, dark green, and orange embroidery floss
scrap of fiberfill batting

HEATHER FRIENDSHIP TAG CUTTING GUIDE

2 white/light green print tags (do not cut until embroidery is completed; see directions)

DIRECTIONS

Trace the tag outline twice on right side of white/light green print fabric. Trace the words, flowers, stems, leaves, and and dots inside one tag. Place the fabric in an embroidery hoop (page 17). Using three strands floss in needle, embroider the words in dark green backstitch, the flower stems in light green backstitch, the leaves in light green satin stitch, the flowers in orange satin stitch, the flower stamens in orange chain stitch, and the dots in orange French knots.

Cut out both tags. Sew white trim around edge of front tag, right sides facing and edges matching; trim off excess. Fold orange ribbon in half. Place folded edge on top edge of tag front at spot marked by × on pattern; baste in place. Roll the free ribbon ends together into a small loop and secure temporarily with a paper clip so they won't accidentally get caught up in the stitching. Place front and back tags together, right sides facing. Stitch all around, catching white trim and folded ribbon in seam; leave an opening in bottom for turning. Turn right side out. Sew closed from back, making tiny stitches. Release ribbon ends from paper clip.

MAY THE HINGES OF OUR FRIENDSHIP NEVER GROW RUSTY

ottage kitchen

fornia S

SHAMROCK SUPPLIES

scraps of green and orange print fabric
scrap of fiberfill batting
green and orange sewing thread
two ¾" bar pins
glue gun

SHAMROCK CUTTING GUIDE

Note: Do not cut pieces until machine stitching is completed; see directions.

2 green print shamrocks
2 orange print shamrocks
2 fiberfill batting shamrocks

SHAMROCK DIRECTIONS

For each shamrock, trace the shamrock pattern once on right side of green or orange print fabric. Place against a piece of matching fabric, wrong sides facing, and slip fiberfill in between. Pin securely. Set the sewing machine for close-set zigzag stitches about ¹⁄₁₆" wide (machine satin stitch). Using matching thread, stitch around edge of shamrock on marked line. Cut away excess fabric and fiberfill with sharp scissors, being careful not to cut stitching thread. Glue bar pin to center back.

Irish Currant Soda Bread

2½ cups all-purpose flour
½ teaspoon salt
2 teaspoons baking soda
3 tablespoons granulated sugar
1 teaspoon baking powder
3 tablespoons butter, chilled
1 cup black currants
¾ cup buttermilk

baking sheet, greased

Preheat oven to 375°F. In a large bowl, sift together flour, salt, baking soda, sugar, and baking powder until well combined. Using a pastry blender or two knives, cut in butter until mixture resembles coarse meal. Mix in currants. Make a well in the center, then pour in buttermilk all at once. Stir quickly with a fork just enough to moisten all ingredients. Turn dough out onto a lightly floured board, form into a ball, and knead four or five times. Form dough into a gently rounded 7-inch-diameter loaf and place on greased baking sheet. Using a sharp knife, cut a large X across the top of the loaf about ¼" deep. Bake for 45 minutes, or until top is golden brown and a testing straw inserted in the center comes out clean.
Makes 1 loaf.

Note: The large cellophane-wrapped loaf in the photograph was made by doubling the recipe.

Pin folded ribbon here
before sewing seam

X

MAY·THE·HINGES

OF·OUR

FRIENDSHIP

NEVER·GROW

RUSTY

● Leave open for turning ●

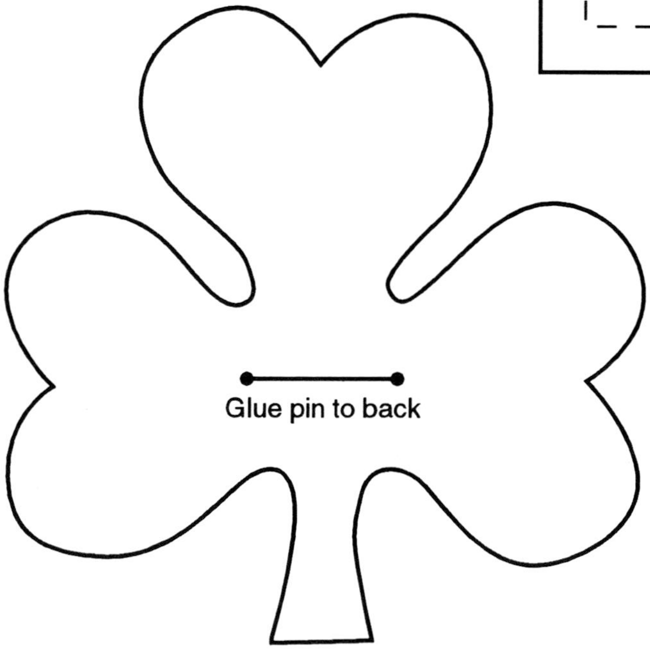

Glue pin to back

Appliquéd Flower Pot

Paint, fabric appliqués, and ribbons are all it takes to turn an ordinary clay flower pot into a blooming beauty. Fill it with ivy or a flowering plant for an attractive Easter gift alternative to cut flowers. If you have a green thumb, you can pot a plant you've sprouted yourself for a present that is truly unique Clay pot is 6" tall; top opening is 8" across.

SUPPLIES

clay flower pot 8" across × 6" high, including 1½" rim
plastic liner to fit pot
white nontoxic spray paint
scraps of white, yellow, pink, and green fabrics
1⅜ yards ½" light blue satin ribbon
⅔ yard ½" pink satin ribbon
scrap of fiberfill batting
glue gun

CUTTING GUIDE

1 white background block (do not cut until appliqué is completed; see directions)
1 yellow flower A
1 pink center B
4 green leaf C's
1 green stem D
1 fiberfill batting block

DIRECTIONS

Spray the flower pot with white paint, following paint manufacturer's directions. Let dry, then spray a second coat. Let dry completely.

Trace the background block and appliqué outlines on right side of white fabric. Prepare yellow flower A, pink flower center B, 4 green leaf C's, and 1 green stem D for appliqué (page 18). Arrange these seven appliqués on the background fabric: Position pink center on yellow flower, slip top of stem under flower, and position two leaves on each side of stem; stem should touch lower marked edge. Appliqué in place. Cut out block. Set block, appliquéd side up, on fiberfill block, and baste. Quilt around flower, stem, and leaves through both layers in outline quilting.

Glue the finished block to the front of the flower pot so top edge of block butts lower edge of pot rim. Cut two 4½" pieces of blue ribbon and glue to sides of block, concealing raw edges. Cut a piece of ribbon to fit around pot just under rim plus 1". Fold one end ½" to wrong side. Glue around pot, lapping folded end over cut end in back. Cut remaining ribbon to fit around pot's lower edge and glue in same way. Cut pink ribbon in half. Tie each piece into a small bow and glue to front of pot at top corners of block. Set plastic liner in pot before you add plant to prevent water from seeping through clay and damaging fabric.

← No seam
allowance needed

Background Block

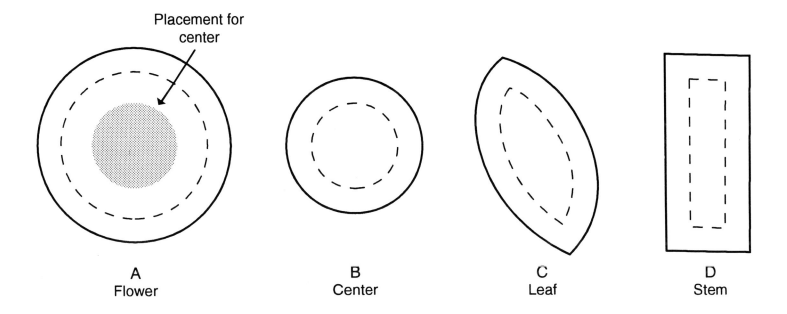

Placement for
center

A
Flower

B
Center

C
Leaf

D
Stem

Patchwork Easter Bunny

This soft, cuddly patchwork bunny with a heart necklace will appeal to children and adults alike. To send bunny off to a new owner, set her in a basket of Easter grass, and snuggle some Carrot Cookies alongside. Each carrot-shaped cookie is decorated with orange and green frosting that is sure to tempt people nibblers too. Bunny is 7" × 7¼"; necklace heart is 1½" × 1½".

SUPPLIES

¼ yard light green striped fabric
scraps of light green print, peach print, and white fabric
½ yard 1⁄16" peach satin ribbon
1 skein each black, white, and green embroidery floss
fiberfill

CUTTING GUIDE

For patchwork block (make 2):
8 light green print A's
8 white A's
4 white B's
1 light green striped B
Additional pieces for bunny:
2 green striped bodies (do not cut until eye embroidery is completed; see directions)
4 peach print ears
1 white tail
1 patchwork heart (assembled from 2 peach print and 2 light green print squares 1½" × 1½"; see directions)
1 peach print heart back

DIRECTIONS

Make two patchwork blocks following Diagram 1. For each block, sew light green print A's and white A's together in pairs along a shorter edge so white triangle is on left (a). Sew 8 A/A triangles together in pairs, matching long edges, for 4 pieced A squares (b). Sew 2 white B's to white edges of a pieced A square to make rows 1 and 3. Sew two remaining pieced A squares to green striped B to make row 2. Sew the three rows together to complete the patchwork block (c).

Trace two bunny bodies (reverse one) on right side of green striped fabric. Trace eye, ear placement line, and block position on both bodies. Place fabric in embroidery hoop (page 17). Using two strands floss in needle, embroider green pupil and white portion of each eye in satin stitch. Using one strand black floss, embroider eye outlines and lashes in backstitch.

Cut out both bodies on marked lines. Prepare patchwork blocks for appliqué (page 18). Appliqué each block in position on bunny body. Place both body pieces together, right sides facing and edges matching. Stitch all around, leaving an opening at bottom for turning. Clip curves and clip in at neck as indicated on pattern. Turn right side out. Stuff firmly with fiberfill. Sew opening closed with tiny stitches.

Make two ears following Diagram 2. Sew ears together in pairs, right sides facing and edges matching; leave short straight edge open. Clip curves, and turn right side out. Fold raw edges ¼" to inside and press (a). Fold corners down until they meet in center, sew butting edges together by hand (b). Place ear on bunny body at an angle (c), matching folded edge to ear placement line, and sew securely with tiny stitches.

Press edge of tail ¼" to wrong side all around. Hand-baste close to fold. Draw up threads until circle starts forming a small pouch. Stuff with fiberfill, draw threads completely closed, and tie off. Sew tail to bunny back seam at spot marked by ✕ on pattern.

Make patchwork heart following Diagram 3. Cut two peach print and two light green print 1½" × 1½" squares. Sew different prints together in pairs, then sew pairs together to make a simple four-patch block (a). Trace heart pattern on block and cut out (b). Place pieced heart and peach print heart back together, right sides facing and edges matching. Stitch all around, leaving a small opening for turning. Turn right side out, stuff firmly, and sew opening closed. Sew midpoint of peach ribbon to back of heart. Tie ribbon around patchwork bunny's neck.

Carrot Cookies

¾ cup margarine, softened at room temperature
1 cup granulated sugar
2 large eggs
1 teaspoon lemon extract
2 drops yellow plus 1 drop red food coloring
2½ cups sifted all-purpose flour
1 teaspoon salt
1 teaspoon baking powder
½ cup carrots, finely shredded

cookie sheets, ungreased

Preheat oven to 400°F. In a large mixing bowl, cream margarine and sugar together until smooth. Add eggs, lemon extract, and food coloring, and mix until well blended. In a medium bowl, sift flour, salt, and baking powder together. Add sifted dry ingredients to the egg mixture gradually, mixing until well combined. Mix in shredded carrot. Shape dough into a ball and chill, covered, in the refrigerator for 1 hour. Turn chilled dough out onto a lightly floured board and roll to a ¼-inch thickness. To make cookies, place carrot template on top of dough and cut around it with a sharp knife dusted with flour. Transfer cookies with a metal spatula to an ungreased cookie sheet, setting them about 1 inch apart. Bake for 6 to 8 minutes, or until lightly brown around the edges. Cool on a wire rack. Using a spatula, spread orange frosting across lower section of each cookie for carrot and spread green frosting across top for carrot top.
Makes about 24 cookies.

Orange and Green Frosting

1 cup confectioners' sugar
1 tablespoon light cream cheese (bar type)
2 tablespoons milk
2 drops yellow plus 1 drop red food coloring
2 drops green food coloring

In a small mixing bowl, mix light cream cheese and milk together. Slowly add confectioners' sugar and continue mixing by hand until firm consistency is reached; if frosting is too stiff to be spreadable, add more milk, 1 teaspoon at a time, and mix thoroughly after each addition. Divide frosting in half, placing each portion into a small bowl. Stir yellow and red food coloring into one portion to make orange frosting, and stir green food coloring into other portion to make green frosting.
Makes ⅓ cup frosting.

Note: Cut carrot template before you begin. Photocopy or trace the Carrot Cookie outline, then tape the copy to lightweight cardboard. Cut on the marked lines to make template.

Diagram 1
Patchwork Block Assembly

(a)

(b)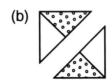

(c)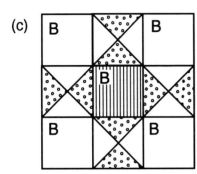

Row 1

Row 2

Row 3

Diagram 2

(a)

(b)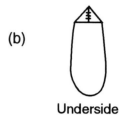

Underside

(c)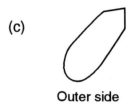

Outer side

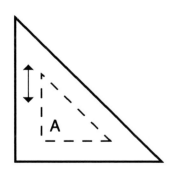

A

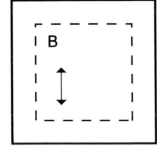

B

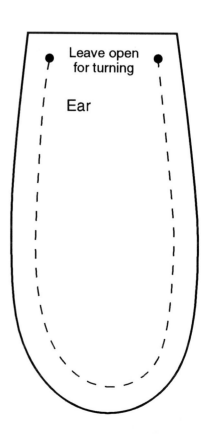

Leave open
for turning

Ear

Diagram 3

(a)

(b)

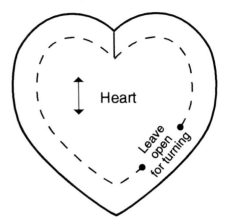

Heart

Leave open for turning

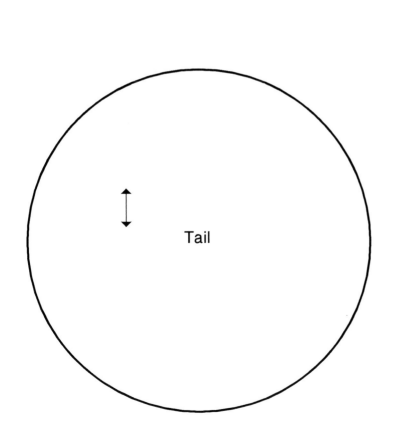

Tail

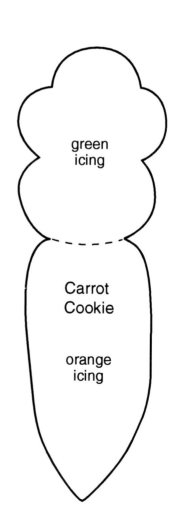

green icing

Carrot Cookie

orange icing

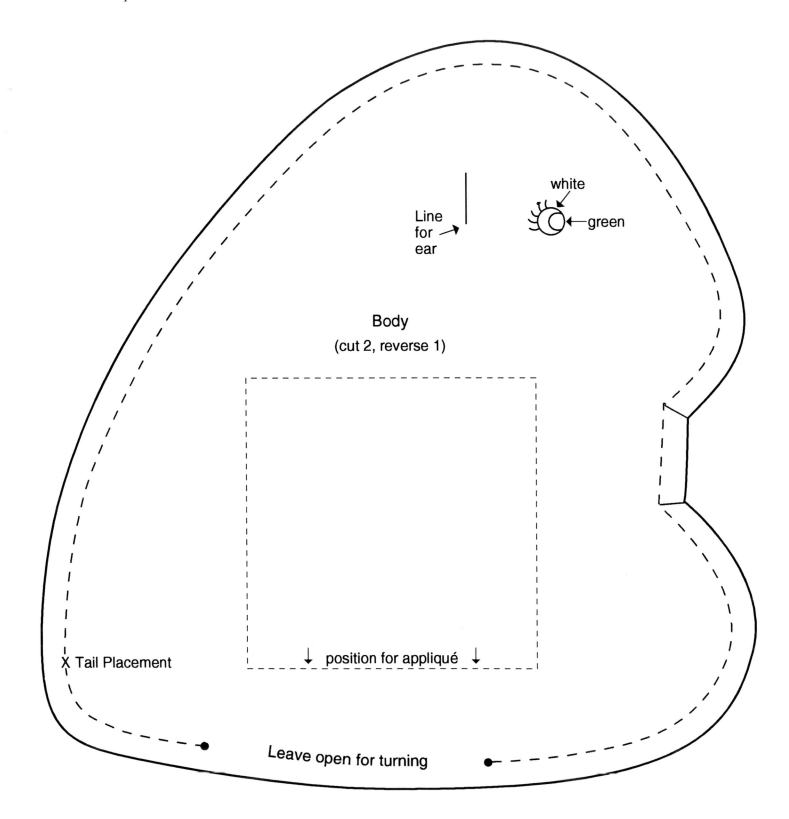

white

Line
for
ear

green

Body

(cut 2, reverse 1)

↓   position for appliqué   ↓

X Tail Placement

Leave open for turning

May Day Basket

When I was a little girl, I delighted to hear my mother's stories of May Day school celebrations in the 1930s, when the Queen of the May and her princesses wove long colorful ribbons in beautiful patterns around the maypole. Years later, while visiting friends in a small town in Iowa, I stumbled upon a midwestern May Day custom. I returned to my hotel to find a delightful little basket of flowers tied to my door. I'd like to keep this charming custom alive, so I created the soft fabric May basket featured here. It is filled with dried and silk flowers, but you could substitute fresh flowers or an edible treat. Finished basket is 4" × 4" × 4", excluding handle.

SUPPLIES

⅛ yard yellow pindot fabric
scraps of white, orange pindot, green pindot, and blue print fabrics
1⅛ yard ¼" white flat eyelet trim
1⅛ yard white 1" single-fold bias tape
fiberfill batting
4" × 4" × 2" florist's foam
mixed bouquet of dried or silk flowers

CUTTING GUIDE

9 yellow pindot A's
1 white A (do not cut until machine appliqué is completed; see directions)
2 orange pindot B's
1 orange pindot heart
2 yellow pindot tulips
2 blue print bluebells
2 green pindot tulip leaves
2 green pindot bluebell leaves
5 fiberfill batting squares 4" × 4"
1 fiberfill batting rectangle 1¼" × 10¼"

DIRECTIONS

Trace block A, and appliqué outlines and stems on right side of white fabric. Prepare heart, tulips, bluebells, and leaves for machine appliqué (page 19). Arrange all pieces on right side of white A and affix with gluestick. Using matching sewing threads, appliqué by machine; machine–satin-stitch over stem lines with green thread. Cut out block A.

Cut four 4½" lengths of eyelet trim. Place one piece against top edge of appliquéd A and remaining pieces against top edge of three yellow pindot A's, right sides facing; baste in place. Set four yellow pindot A's on top, right sides facing and edges matching. Sew ¼" from edge across top of each block through all layers.

Fold the four A units right side out. Slip a batting square in between the two fabrics of each unit, and baste around edges. Quilt around heart and flowers on white A in outline quilting. Following the Assembly Diagram, sew units together at sides,

wrong sides facing; seams will appear on the out-side (a). Sew fourth seam to complete the dimensional block shape (b). Using white bias tape, bind the edges (page 19), turning under ends at top of basket for a neat finish.

To make bottom of basket, place two remaining yellow pindot A's together, wrong sides facing. Slip remaining batting square in between, and baste around edges. Turn basket inside out. Pin bottom to basket, right sides facing and raw edges matching. Sew edges together, then bind with tape. Turn basket right side out, so bottom binding is on inside of basket.

Cut two 10¼" lengths of eyelet trim. Place on long edges of one B handle, right sides facing. Machine-stitch ¼" from edges. Press seam allowances to wrong side. Press long edges of second B handle ¼" to wrong side. Place two B's together, wrong sides facing. Slip batting rectangle in between. Hand-sew long edges together at back, making tiny stitches. Fold raw edges at each end ¼" to inside and press. Sew handle ends to inside of basket at sides.

Insert florist's foam into basket. Stick stems of dried or silk flowers into foam.

Assembly Diagram

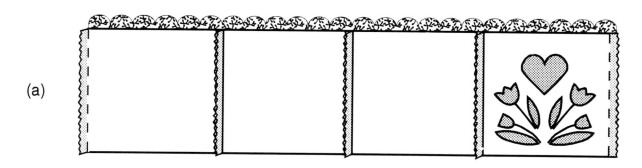

(a)

(b)

A

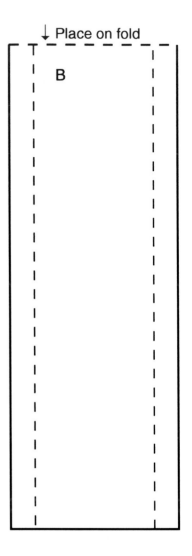

↓ Place on fold

B

"Love to Mom"
Gift Bag and Tag

I decorated this bag just for my mother, Lila, who loves the soft restful colors of pink and blue. The patchwork house is worked in muted shades, but you can choose any color scheme that your mother would enjoy. A coordinating heart tag ties to the handle for gift-giving; Mom can slip it onto a knob or hang it on the wall for a lasting reminder of the love you share. My mom laughingly admits to having a sweet tooth, so I tucked a double batch of Easy Peanut Butter Chocolate Candy (my favorite recipe in the entire book!) inside. The gift bag is 8" × 9½"; patchwork house block is 6" × 6"; heart tag is about 5½" across.

GIFT BAG SUPPLIES

8" × 9½" purchased blue gift bag
scraps of muslin, pink, blue print, and
    pink/blue/cream print fabrics
1½ yards ¼" cream cotton lace trim
scrap of fiberfill batting
glue gun

GIFT BAG CUTTING GUIDE

2 muslin A's
1 muslin B
2 blue print B's
2 muslin C's
1 pink/blue/cream print D
1 pink/blue/cream print F
2 pink/blue/cream print G's
1 pink/blue/cream print H
1 pink E
2 pink G's

GIFT BAG DIRECTIONS

Make house block following House Patchwork Diagram. Sew muslin A, B, and A together alternately with blue B's to make row 1. Sew pink/blue/cream print D to pink E, then sew a muslin C to each end to make row 2. Sew 2 pink G's together along long edges, then sew 2 print G's to each outside long edge. Sew print F horizontally to top edge. Sew print H to F/G edge to make row 3. Sew the three rows together to complete house patchwork block. The block should measure 6½" × 6½".

    Press raw edges of block ¼" to wrong side. Glue lace trim to wrong side of block, so lace protrudes beyond folded edge all around. Glue block to center front of bag. Glue remaining lace to inside top edge of bag so lace extends beyond edge.

TAG SUPPLIES

scraps of muslin and pink/blue/cream print fabric
¾ yard ¹⁄₁₆" blue satin ribbon
⅝ yard blue piping
1 skein blue embroidery floss

TAG CUTTING GUIDE

1 muslin inner heart (do not cut until embroidery is
   completed; see directions)
2 pink/blue/cream print outer hearts
1 fiberfill batting heart without seam allowance

TAG DIRECTIONS

Trace the inner heart outline and script on right
side of muslin. Place the fabric in an embroidery
hoop (page 17). Using two strands blue floss in
needle, embroider script in backstitch.

Cut out embroidered inner heart on marked line
and prepare it for appliqué (page 18). Center
embroidered heart on one outer heart and appliqué
in place. Sew piping around appliquéd outer heart,
butting ends for a neat finish (page 19). Place front
and back outer hearts together, right sides facing
and edges matching. Stitch all around, securing
piping in seam; leave an opening for turning. Clip
curves, bottom point, and top center. Turn right
side out. Insert fiberfill heart into opening and
maneuver so it fills out the shape. Sew opening
closed, making tiny stitches. Quilt around inner
heart appliqué in outline quilting.

Cut a 12" length from ribbon. Tie into a bow
and tack to top of front heart. Fold remaining ribbon in half, and tie an overhand knot at midpoint.
Position knot on back of heart just below center
top and sew in place. Tie ribbon ends around handle of gift bag.

Easy Peanut Butter Chocolate Candy

2 cups (4 sticks) butter, softened at room
   temperature
4 cups creamy peanut butter
1 teaspoon vanilla extract
6 cups confectioners' sugar
3 6-oz. bags semisweet chocolate chips
¾ cup sweetened condensed milk
½ cup walnuts, finely chopped, in a small bowl

baking sheet lined with wax paper

In a medium-sized mixing bowl, cream the butter,
peanut butter, and vanilla extract together until light
brown and smooth. Add the confectioners' sugar gradually and mix until peanut butter mixture is stiff and
separates from the bowl. Roll into 1-inch balls, insert a
toothpick into each ball, and set on a baking sheet lined
with wax paper. Melt the chocolate chips in a double
boiler. Stir in milk gradually, blending well until
chocolate reaches a creamy consistency; if chocolate
mixture is too thick, add more milk, 1 tablespoon at a
time, blending thoroughly after each addition. Holding
each ball by its toothpick, dip it into chocolate mixture,
roll it in the chopped nuts until coated all around, then
set it back on the wax paper. Chill in refrigerator ½
hour, or until chocolate is set.
Makes about 36 candies.

House Patchwork Diagram

Row 1

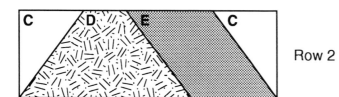

Row 2

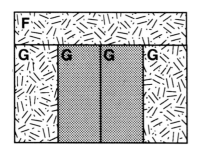

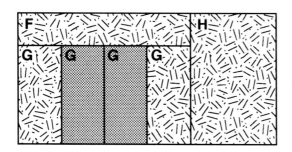

Row 3

Completed Block

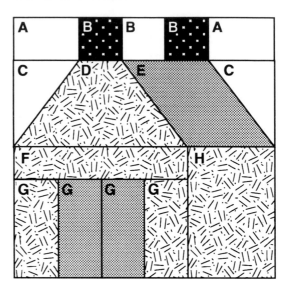

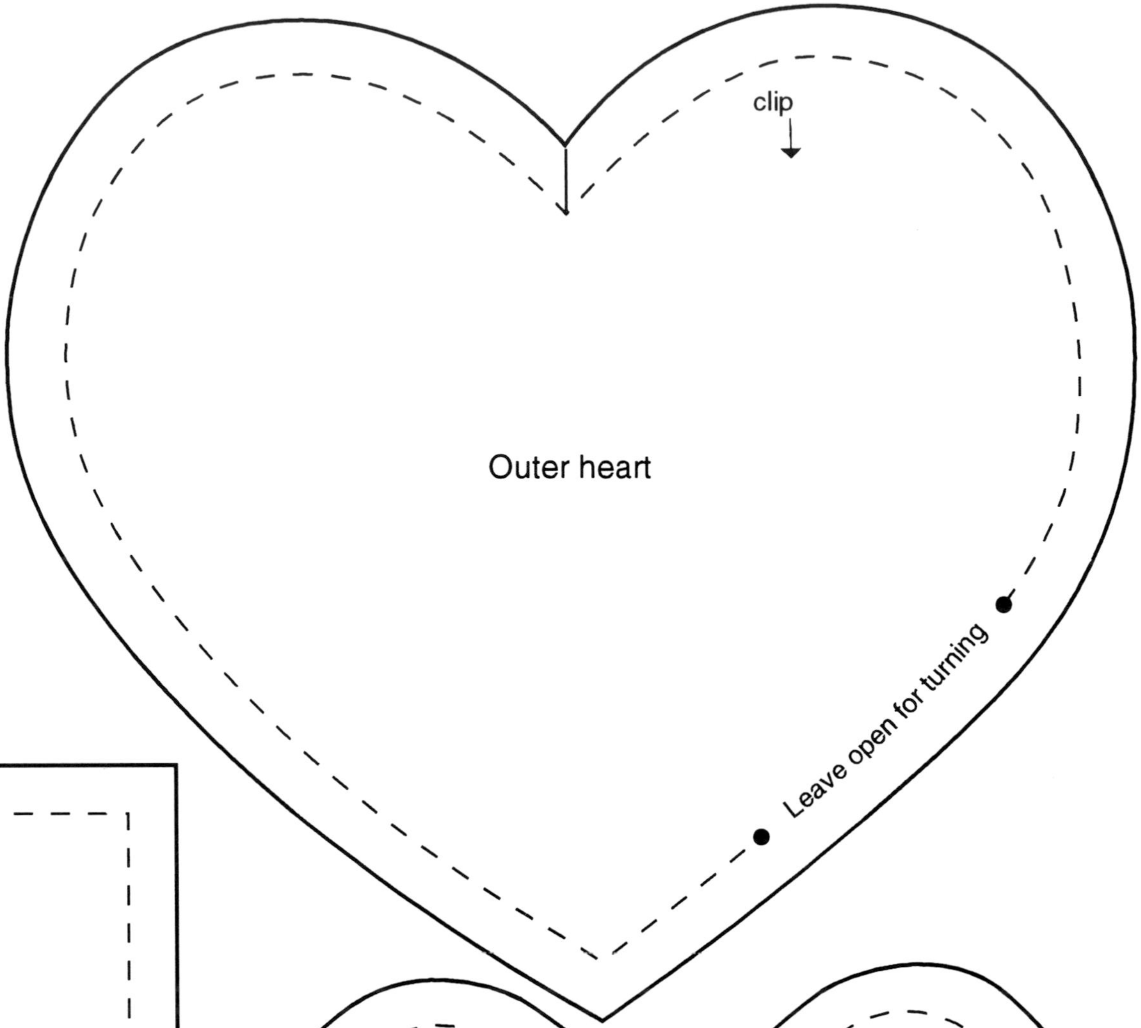

clip

Outer heart

Leave open for turning

H

Love
to
Mom

Inner heart

"Bow Tie"
Gift Bag and Tag

I know Dad's Favorite Lemon Cupcakes will be as popular with your dad as they were with mine. Whip up a special Father's Day batch just for him, then deliver them in a gift package trimmed with a patchwork bow tie. Even if he's hardly ever sentimental, he'll treasure the keepsake "Love to Dad" tag tied on the handles. Gift bag is 7¾" × 9"; bow tie patchwork is 6" × 6"; gift tag is 3" × 3".

GIFT BAG SUPPLIES

7¾" × 9" purchased blue gift bag
scraps of muslin, navy blue print, and brown print
   fabrics
¾ yard navy blue piping
glue gun

GIFT BAG CUTTING GUIDE

2 muslin A's
2 navy blue print A's
1 brown print B
2 brown print C strips 1½" × 4½"
2 brown print D strips 1½" × 6½"

GIFT BAG DIRECTIONS

Make bow tie block following diagram. Sew muslin A's and navy blue print A's together in pairs for 2 A/A rectangles (a). Sew rectangles together so adjacent fabrics contrast (b). Prepare brown print B for appliqué (page 18). Center B on point on pieced A block and appliqué in place (c). Frame the block by sewing 2 brown print C strips to top and bottom edges, then 2 brown print D strips to side edges. Block should measure 6½" × 6½".

  Sew piping around edge of block, butting ends for a neat finish (page 19). Press raw edges of block ¼" to wrong side. Glue finished block to center front of bag on point, so navy blue bow tie is horizontal.

TAG SUPPLIES

scrap of muslin fabric
⅜ yard navy blue piping
½ yard ½" blue satin ribbon
 1 skein navy blue embroidery floss
scrap of fiberfill batting

TAG CUTTING GUIDE

2 muslin tags (do not cut until embroidery is
   completed; see directions)
1 fiberfill batting tag without seam allowance

TAG DIRECTIONS

Trace the tag outline twice on right side of muslin.
Trace the script inside one tag. Place the muslin in
an embroidery hoop (page 17). Using two strands
navy blue floss in needle, embroider the script in
backstitch.

Cut out both tags on the marked lines. Sew piping around edge of front tag, butting ends for a
neat finish (page 19). Fold ribbon in half. Place
folded edge of ribbon against top edge of tag front
at spot marked by ✕ on pattern; baste in place.
Roll the free ribbon ends together into a small loop
and secure temporarily with a paper clip so they
won't accidentally get caught up in the stitching.
Place front and back tags together, right sides facing
and edges matching.   Stitch all around, securing
piping and ribbon in seam; leave an opening on
side for turning. Turn right side out. Insert batting into opening and maneuver so it fills out the
shape. Sew closed from back, making tiny stitches.
Quilt all around outer edge ¼" from piping.
Release ribbon ends from paper clip and tie to bag
handles.

Dad's Favorite Lemon Cupcakes

1 package 2-layer lemon cake mix
1 3-oz. package lemon-flavored gelatin
3 large eggs
⅓ cup vegetable oil
1 cup water
1 teaspoon lemon extract

2¾" fluted muffin pans and cupcake liners

Preheat oven to 350°F. In a medium mixing bowl,
combine cake mix, gelatin, eggs, oil, water, and lemon
extract, and beat at medium speed for 2 to 3 minutes.
Spoon batter evenly into lined muffin cups about two-
thirds full.   Bake for 20 minutes, or until lightly
browned and risen to top of liners. Let cool thoroughly in pan, then set individual cupcakes on a plate. Frost
with Lemon-Orange Icing.
Makes 24 cupcakes.

Lemon-Orange Icing

¼ cup butter, softened at room temperature
2 cups confectioners' sugar
¼ cup orange juice
1 teaspoon lemon extract

In a medium mixing bowl, cream butter and a few
tablespoons of the confectioners' sugar together until
smooth. Add remaining sugar alternately with orange
juice and lemon extract and continue beating until
smooth.
Makes 1⅓ cups.

Bow Tie Block Diagram

 (a)

 (b)

 (c)

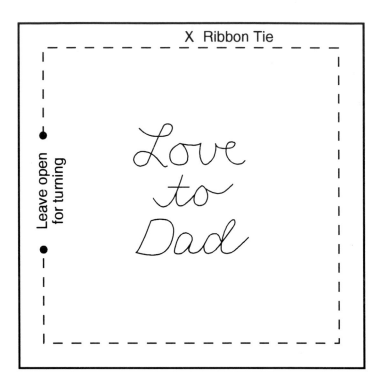

X Ribbon Tie

Leave open
for turning

*Love
to
Dad*

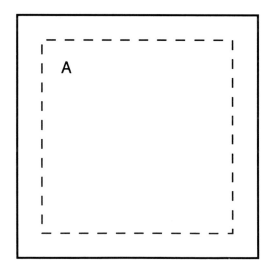

A

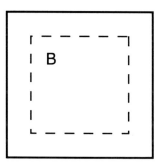

B

Patriotic Basket and Jar Toppers

The miniature red, white, and blue swags on this dessert basket recall the yards of bunting that decorated yesteryear's Fourth of July grandstands and gazebos. To celebrate a grand old-fashioned "4th" with family and friends, I pack the basket with summer shortcake fixin's in jars with patriotic toppers. Each serving is assembled right on the plate, using three kinds of summer berries and crème fraîche. Basket is 7" high × 8" across; jar toppers are 7½" in diameter, to fit jars 3½" across.

BASKET SUPPLIES

round wicker basket 8" across × 7" high, plus
    handle
white nontoxic spray paint
¼ yard red/white striped fabric
scrap of navy blue fabric
½ yard ½" red grosgrain ribbon
½ yard ¼" navy blue grosgrain ribbon
purchased 1¼" embroidered star appliqué
covered button kit to make four 1½" buttons
glue gun

BASKET CUTTING GUIDE

4 red/white striped rectangles 4" × 18" (cut so
    stripes run parallel to 4" edges)

BASKET DIRECTIONS

Spray the basket with white paint, following paint manufacturer's directions. Let dry, then spray a second coat. Let dry completely.

Press one long edge of each red/white striped rectangle ¼" to wrong side. Topstitch close to fold. Make two parallel rows of machine-basting ³⁄₁₆" and ⁵⁄₁₆" from remaining long raw edge. Pull bobbin threads and gather as tightly as possible. Press short raw edges ¼" to wrong side.

Glue swags end to end around outside rim of basket as pictured in photograph. Make four navy blue covered buttons following package directions. Glue each button to center of a swag, concealing gathering stitches. Lay navy blue ribbon on top of red ribbon, and tie both ribbons together into a bow. Glue to center front of basket, between two swags. Glue embroidered star on top, concealing knot.

JAR TOPPERS SUPPLIES

For 2 toppers:
¼ yard white/blue print fabric
1⅜ yards ¼" red/white/blue striped grosgrain ribbon
1⅜ yards 1" red pregathered satin ribbon
purchased ⅞" embroidered star appliqué
2 small snaps
compass

JAR TOPPERS CUTTING GUIDE

2 white/blue print 7½"-diameter circles (see directions)

JAR TOPPERS DIRECTIONS

Using a compass, draw two 7½"-diameter circles on white/blue print fabric. Cut out on marked lines. For each topper, pin the gathered edge of the red ribbon against edge of circle, right sides facing; fold and overlap the ends and trim off the excess. Sew ¼" from edge all around. Fold ribbon down so seam turns to wrong side. Topstitch through all layers close to fold.

For each jar, cut a length of striped ribbon to go around jar lid once plus 1". Fold ends ¼" to wrong side and tack by hand. Separate snap into male and female pieces. Sew male snap to one end of ribbon on wrong side; sew female snap to other end of ribbon on right side, allowing for a ½" overlap. Fold striped jar band in half and mark midpoint with a pin. Cut a 17" length of striped ribbon, tie into a bow, and sew to midpoint of jar band. Glue embroidered star on top, concealing knot.

To use toppers, fill jars and screw on lids. Center toppers on lids and secure with a rubber band around each rim. Wrap striped jar bands around rims, concealing rubber bands, and snap in back.

Summer Shortcake with Crème Fraîche

Shortcake

- 2 cups sifted all-purpose flour
- 3 tablespoons granulated sugar
- 3 teaspoons baking powder
- 1 teaspoon salt
- ⅓ cup margarine, chilled
- 1 cup buttermilk

9" square baking pan, greased

Preheat oven to 400°F. In a medium-sized bowl, sift together flour, sugar, baking powder, and salt. Using a pastry blender or two knives, cut in margarine until mixture resembles coarse meal. Make a well in the center, then pour in buttermilk all at once. Stir quickly with a fork just enough to moisten all ingredients. Turn mixture into pan, and pat into edges and corners. Bake 15 to 20 minutes, or until golden brown. Let cool, then cut into 4 squares.

Berry Topping

- 2 cups fresh or frozen strawberries
- 2 cups fresh or frozen blackberries
- 2 cups fresh or frozen raspberries
- 1 cup granulated sugar (add more sugar if berries are extremely tart)

Wash and hull fresh berries; thaw frozen berries and let drain. Cut strawberries in half. Place all berries in a large mixing bowl, and fold in sugar until berries are evenly coated. Let stand for 1 to 2 hours, or until sugar is absorbed. Refrigerate until ready to serve.
Makes 6 cups.

Crème Fraîche

- 1 cup heavy cream
- 1 cup sour cream

Whisk the heavy cream and sour cream together in a medium-sized nonmetallic bowl. Lay plastic wrap loosely over the top without forming a seal. Let stand at room temperature overnight for up to 24 hours; do not place in direct sunlight. Cover and chill in refrigerator for 4 hours to develop the characteristic tangy flavor.
Makes 2 cups.

To serve shortcake: Fork-split each shortcake square horizontally and place lower half on dessert plate. Spoon a generous helping of berry topping on top. Place top half of shortcake on berries, add more berry topping, and finish with a dollop of crème fraîche.
Makes 4 servings.

Happy Haunting Trick-or-Treat Bag

Like most children, I started planning my Halloween costume weeks in advance, and when the haunted night finally arrived, I raced through my dinner so I could start on my neighborhood trick-or-treating right away! Today's trick-or-treaters can enjoy Popcorn Pumpkins—traditional popcorn balls decorated with bits of black gumdrops and licorice so they look like jack-o'-lanterns. Use the ghostly treat bag to hold goodies for trick-or-treaters that come to your door, or stitch up a few for young goblins to take on their Halloween rounds. Bag is 10¼" × 13½". The black tote bag and mini muffins are described on page 153.

SUPPLIES

⅛ yard orange/white dotted fabric
scrap of white fabric
⅔ yard white eyelet beading (for ¼" ribbon insertion) with attached ½" eyelet ruffle along one edge
1 yard ¼" black picot-edged satin ribbon
1 skein black embroidery floss

CUTTING GUIDE

2 orange/white dotted bags (do not cut until embroidery is completed; see directions)
2 white ghosts (do not cut until embroidery is completed; see directions)

DIRECTIONS

Complete the bag pattern by joining bag A on page 151 and bag B on page 152. Trace two bags on orange/white dot fabric. Trace the words **Happy Haunting** on the right side of the bag front 1¾" above the bottom edge. Place fabric in embroidery hoop (page 17). Using three strands black floss in needle, embroider words in backstitch.

Trace two ghosts on right side of white fabric, marking one on the cutting line and one on the stitching line. Trace the face on the ghost that includes the seam allowance. Place fabric in embroidery hoop. Using two strands black floss in needle, embroider eye outlines, lashes, nose, and mouth in backstitch and pupils in satin stitch.

Prepare the embroidered ghost for appliqué (page 18), placing smaller ghost cutout on top of paper template to prevent "see-through." Appliqué ghost to bag front above embroidered lettering. For extra stiffness, do not remove paper template.

Place bag front and back together, right sides facing and edges matching. Stitch sides and bottom; leave top edge open. Turn right side out. Press top edge ¼" to wrong side twice. Topstitch ³⁄₁₆" from edge all around. Pin white eyelet beading around top of bag so ruffled edge extends beyond top folded edge of bag; fold and overlap ends for a neat finish. Topstitch all around on each edge of beading. Thread black ribbon through beading. Pull ribbon ends to draw up top of bag into gathers, and tie in a bow. Knot ends of ribbon streams to prevent raveling.

A TREAT FOR YOU

Happy Haunting

Popcorn Pumpkins

 5 quarts freshly popped popcorn
 2 cups granulated sugar
1½ cups water
 ½ teaspoon salt
 ½ cup light corn syrup
 1 tablespoon vinegar
 1 tablespoon vanilla extract
25 drops red plus 15 drops yellow food coloring
3-4 black licorice sticks
36 black gumdrops

Place popcorn in a large ovenproof bowl and set in a 300°F oven to keep it hot and crisp. In a medium saucepan, combine sugar, water, salt, corn syrup, and vinegar. Stir continuously over a low heat until sugar melts, then bring to a boil and continue boiling until candy thermometer reaches 250°F. Remove from heat and stir in the vanilla extract and the red and yellow food coloring until well blended. Test color by dipping a single popped kernel into the mixture—it should appear bright orange. If the color is too light, add more red food coloring, 1 drop at a time, and retest color after each addition. Remove popcorn from oven, pour orange mixture over hot popcorn, and mix well with a wooden spoon to coat every kernel. Mold popcorn into 36 3-inch-diameter balls with your hands. Cut 18¾" sections from licorice sticks, then slice each section in half vertically. Stick a vertical stem into each popcorn ball for pumpkin stem. Using a sharp knife, cut a ¼-inch-thick slice off bottom of each gumdrop. Referring to Cutting Diagram, cut two eyes and a nose from each slice. Cut 1-inch sections from remaining licorice, then cut into ⅛-inch strips for mouths. Referring to color photograph, press eyes, nose, and mouth into place on each popcorn ball while still warm.
Makes 36 popcorn balls.

Ghost

Happy Haunting

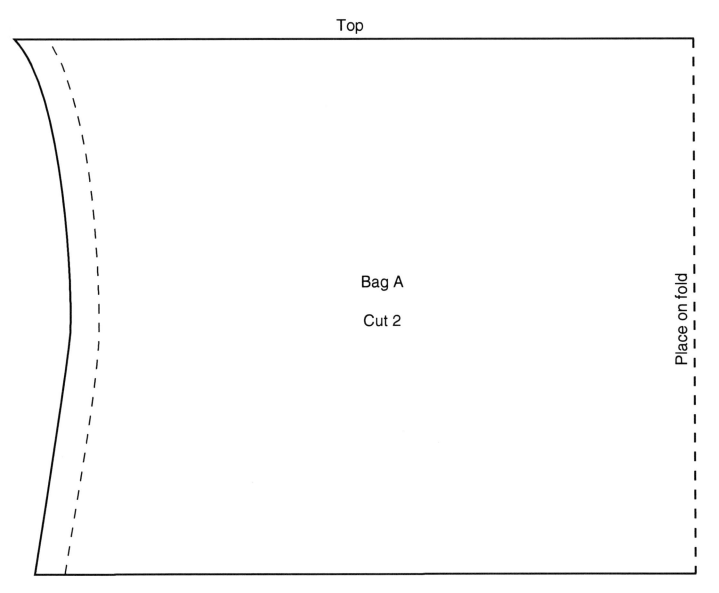

Top

Bag A

Cut 2

Place on fold

Cut pattern on the line and tape to Bag B before cutting fabric.

Line up edge of Bag A on the broken line and tape it in place.

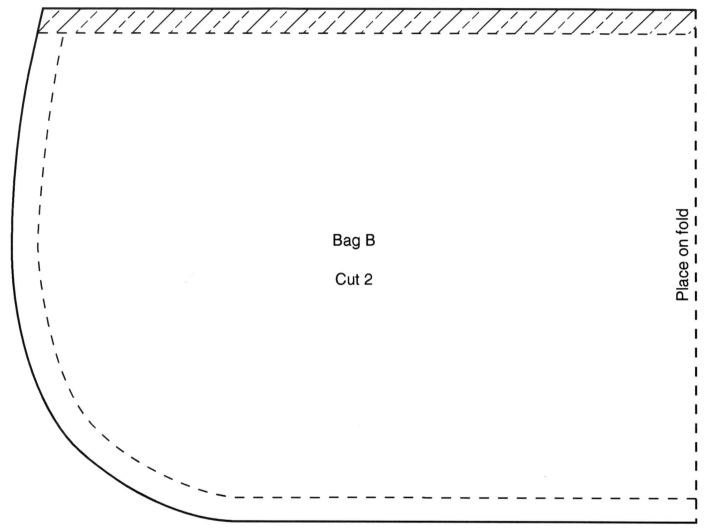

Bag B

Cut 2

Place on fold

Cutting Diagram

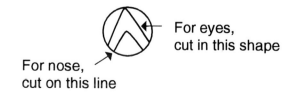

For eyes,
cut in this shape

For nose,
cut on this line

"A Treat for You" Gift Bag

Adults who like Halloween will want to carry this sophisticated fall bag to all their favorite haunts. The crisp black and white design features two mini Churn Dash blocks, an embroidered pumpkin, and a surprise orange lining. Sew it for a friend with a birthday on or near Halloween. Packed inside are Candy Corn Mini Muffins, a spicy pumpkin treat for all ages. Tote is 9" × 9".

SUPPLIES

⅓ yard black print fabric
⅓ yard orange print fabric
scraps of black/white dotted, black/white striped, and white fabrics
⅝ yard white piping
1 skein each black, green, brown, and orange embroidery floss
fiberfill batting

CUTTING GUIDE

For each Churn Dash block (make 2):
1 black/white striped A
4 black/white striped B's
4 black/white dotted B's
4 black/white striped C's
4 black/white dotted C's
Additional pieces for bag:
1 white D (do not cut until embroidery is completed; see directions)
2 black print E's
1 black print back 9½" × 9½"
2 orange print linings 9½" × 9½"
2 fiberfill batting squares 9½" × 9½"
1 black/white dot strip 3½" × 18"
1 fiberfill batting strip 1½" × 18"

DIRECTIONS

Make two miniature Churn Dash blocks following Churn Dash Block Diagram. For each block, sew striped and dotted B's together in pairs for 4 B/B squares (a). Sew striped and dotted C's together in pairs for 4 C/C squares (b). Join two C/C squares to sides of a B/B square to make rows 1 and 3; arrange so each long edge of completed row is in matching fabric. Sew remaining B/B squares to sides of A to make row 2. Join the three rows together. Each completed block should measure 3½" × 3½".

Trace D outline, words, and pumpkin with vine on right side of white fabric. Place fabric in embroidery hoop. Using two strands floss in needle, embroider words in black backstitch, vines and tendril in green backstitch, leaves in green satin stitch, pumpkin in orange satin stitch, stem in brown satin stitch, and pumpkin ridges in brown backstitch. Cut out embroidered D on marked lines. To assemble tote front, sew a mini Churn Dash block to each side edge of embroidered D. Sew 2 black print E's to top and bottom edges. Finished tote front should measure 9½" × 9½".

Lay tote front on top of a batting square and baste with long, loose stitches. Quilt striped A's, B's, and C's and white D in outline quilting. Quilt E's ¼" from seams. Remove all basting threads. Place tote front and back together, right sides facing and edges matching. Place remaining batting square on tote back, and pin all around. Carefully stitch side and bottom edges together, catching batting in seam; leave top edge open. Trim batting close to stitching, clip corners, and turn right side out. Sew piping around top edge of tote, butting edges for a neat finish (page 20).   Sew linings together in same manner as tote; do not turn.   Press top edge of lining ¼" to wrong side.

To make tote handles, press one long edge of 3½" × 18" strip ¼" to wrong side.   Lay strip on a flat surface, wrong side up, and center batting strip on top.   Fold fabric around batting, overlapping raw edge ¼" in center; pin in place.   Topstitch along folded edge through all layers, securing fabric to batting.   Cut strip in half, for two 9" handles.   Pin handles, right sides facing and edges matching, to tote front and back 2" in from side seams.   Stitch ¼" from edge over previous stitching.   Trim batting on wrong side close to stitching.   Press tote top edge to wrong side along stitching line so handles and piping pop up.

Insert the lining into the bag between front and back batting, matching seams and folds.   Hand-sew the lining to the tote along the top inside edge, concealing piping machine stitching.

Candy Corn Mini Muffins

  2 large eggs
1¼ cups granulated sugar
 ⅓ cup vegetable oil
 ½ teaspoon salt
 1 cup cooked pumpkin
 1 teaspoon ground cinnamon
 1 teaspoon ground cloves
 ½ cup water
1¾ cups sifted all-purpose flour
1½ teaspoons baking powder
 ½ teaspoon baking soda
 1 6-oz. package candy corn

1¾" muffin pans, greased

Preheat oven to 375°F.   In a medium-sized bowl, combine eggs, sugar, oil, salt, pumpkin, spices, and water until well blended and light orange.   In a large bowl, sift together flour, baking powder, and baking soda.   Pour in pumpkin mixture and stir just until all ingredients are moistened; batter will be lumpy.   Spoon batter into greased muffin pans until each cup is two-thirds full.   Bake for 15 minutes, or until tops are browned and muffins pull away slightly from edges of pan.   Remove from oven and press a candy corn gently into the soft top of each muffin while still hot.   Let cool in pans for 10 minutes before transferring to a plate.
Makes 36 mini muffins.

Churn Dash Block Diagram

Pieced B block (a)
(make 4)

Pieced C block (b)
(make 4)

Row 1  (c)

Row 2

Row 3

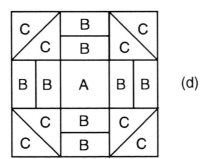 (d)

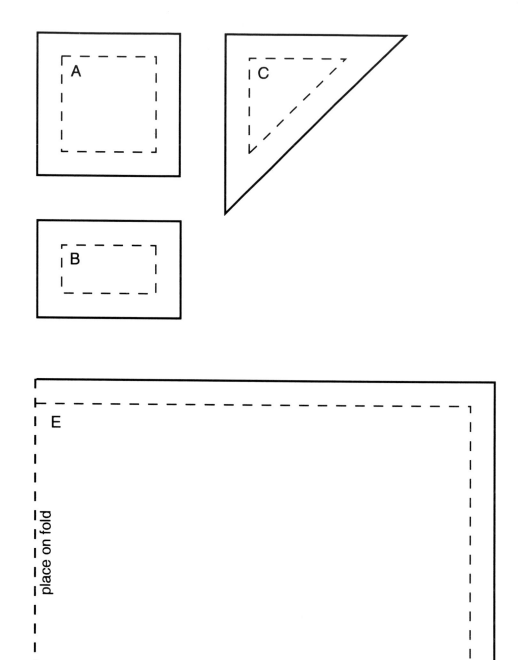

Friendship Baking Dish Cover

Fit this friendship cover over the baked dessert you bring to the clan's next Thanksgiving feast, and watch your hostess smile her gratitude. Patchwork decorates the top of the cover, and a hidden elastic band ensures a snug fit around your baking dish. Shown here are Pumpkin Squares, a satisfying alternative to pumpkin pie. I sampled my first square at a camp one fall, and the cook graciously shared her recipe. Cover fits an 11" × 7" baking pan.

SUPPLIES

½ yard dark green print fabric
scraps of cream, medium rust/white print, dark rust/white print, and dark rust/white dotted fabrics
⅔ yard ½" cream pregathered eyelet trim
1 skein each dark green, dark rust, and gold embroidery floss
½ yard ¼" elastic

CUTTING GUIDE

1 dark green print rectangle (to cut, see directions)
1 cream background (do not cut until embroidery and appliqué are completed; see directions)
1 cream A (do not cut until embroidery is completed; see directions)
4 medium rust/white print A's
4 dark rust/white print A's
4 dark rust/white dotted B's
4 dark green print B's

DIRECTIONS

To custom-cut baking dish cover, lay green print fabric wrong side up on a flat surface. Set clean, empty baking dish face down on fabric. Measure and mark 5" from dish edge all around. Round off the corners by tracing around the edge of a small plate. Cut out cover on marked line. Press the edge ¼" to the wrong side all around. Machine-baste along fold around each corner. Fold edge ½" to wrong side again, pulling up bobbin threads to ease corners. Machine-stitch along first fold to create casing; leave a ⅝" opening along one straight edge to insert elastic.

Trace background outline, patchwork outlines, words, curved lines, and circles on right side of cream fabric. In a separate area of cream fabric, trace 1 block A with small heart in center. Place fabric in embroidery hoop. Using two strands floss in needle, embroider words and curved lines in dark green backstitch, circles in dark rust satin stitch, and heart in gold satin stitch. Cut out block A only.

Make patchwork blocks following Placement Diagram. Sew two medium rust/white print A's to sides of embroidered heart A. Sew four dark rust/white print A's to sides of two remaining medium rust/white print A's. Sew rows together to make 1 pieced A block 3" × 3" with heart in the center. Sew dark rust/white dotted B's and dark green print B's together in pairs for 4 pieced B blocks. Prepare pieced A block and 4 pieced B blocks for appliqué (page 18). Appliqué in position on embroidered cream background.

Cut out cream background on marked line. Pin the eyelet trim to the background, right sides facing and edges matching; fold and overlap the ends for a neat finish, trimming off any excess. Sew ¼" from edge all around. Fold raw edges to wrong side and press. Center the piece on right side of green print cover and pin. Sew securely in place from wrong side with tiny stitches. Thread elastic through casing. Test-fit cover on baking dish, cut elastic shorter if necessary, and sew ends together. Sew casing opening closed with tiny stitches. For gift-giving, seal the baking dish contents with plastic wrap, then slip the fabric cover on top.

Pumpkin Squares

Bottom Layer:
1 package 2-layer yellow cake mix (reserve 1 cup cake mix for topping)
½ cup (1 stick) butter or margarine, melted
1 medium egg

11" × 7" × 1½" baking pan, greased

Filling:
1 lb. canned solid pack (unseasoned) pumpkin
2 large eggs
¾ cup brown sugar
2½ teaspoons pumpkin pie spice

Topping:
¼ cup butter or margarine
¼ cup brown sugar
1 teaspoon ground cinnamon
1 cup yellow cake mix

Preheat oven to 350°F. In a medium mixing bowl, mix cake mix (except 1 cup reserved for topping), melted butter or margarine, and egg until well blended. Press the mixture into greased pan with your fingertips. In a medium bowl, combine canned pumpkin, eggs, brown sugar, and spice and mix with a wooden spoon until well blended. Pour filling in pan over cake mix layer. In a small bowl, combine butter or margarine, brown sugar, cinnamon, and reserved cake mix with your fingers until it becomes crumbly. Sprinkle evenly over filling. Bake for 45 to 50 minutes, or until a testing straw inserted in center comes out clean. Let cool in pan. Cut into 2" × 3½" pieces and serve on individual plates topped with a dollop of whipped cream. *Makes 12 servings.*

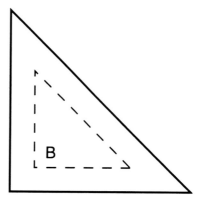

Background/Placement Diagram

Pilgrim Gift Bag

An easy-to-appliqué pilgrim's hat makes a purchased gift bag extra special for Thanksgiving. The hat panel features a gold metallic buckle and embroidered greeting. Preserved oak leaves purchased at a florist shop add textural interest. Inside is a double batch of Molasses Sugar Cookies, a favorite autumn treat and the very first cookie recipe I learned to bake as a child! Bag is 7" × 10".

SUPPLIES

7" × 10" purchased gift bag in autumn colors
scraps of white, black, light brown, and gold
   metallic fabrics
⅔ yard ½" gold metallic braid
1 skein rust embroidery floss
4 preserved oak leaves (available at florist's supply
   stores)
glue gun

CUTTING GUIDE

1 white rectangle 5" × 7¼" (do not cut until
   embroidery and appliqué are completed; see
   directions)
1 black hat
1 light brown hatband
1 gold metallic buckle
2 7¼" gold braid strips
2 5" gold braid strips

DIRECTIONS

Mark 5" × 7½" rectangle on right side of white fabric. Mark a guideline ¾" from bottom edge of block. Trace the words **Happy Thanksgiving** on the guideline, evenly spaced on each side. Place fabric in embroidery hoop (page 17). Using two strands rust embroidery floss in needle, embroider words in backstitch.

Prepare hat, hatband, and buckle for appliqué (page 18). Referring to photograph and pilgrim hat pattern for placement, arrange these three pieces within white rectangle. Appliqué in place.

Cut out white embroidered and appliquéd panel on marked line. Glue panel to front of gift bag, so lower edge is 1" above lower edge of bag. Cut a second white rectangle as a lining if necessary to prevent "see-through." Glue long metallic braid strips to top and bottom of panel. Glue short metallic strips to sides. Glue leaves to top at right and left sides.

Molasses Sugar Cookies

1½ cups (3 sticks) butter
1 cup granulated sugar
1 cup brown sugar
½ cup dark molasses
2 large eggs
4 cups sifted all-purpose flour
4 teaspoons baking soda
1 teaspoon salt
2 teaspoons ground cinnamon
1 teaspoon ground cloves
1 teaspoon ground ginger
small dish of granulated sugar

cookie sheets, greased

Preheat oven to 375°F. Place butter in a 3-quart saucepan and melt over a low heat. Remove from heat and let cool to room temperature. Add sugars, molasses, and eggs and stir until well blended. Sift together flour, baking soda, salt, and spices and add gradually to butter mixture, blending well after each addition. Mixture will appear runny. Chill in a covered container in refrigerator for ½ hour. Form chilled dough into 1-inch balls, roll in sugar to coat, then set balls 2 inches apart on greased cookie sheet. Bake 8 to 10 minutes, or until cookies are flat and cracks in top surface are no longer glossy.
Makes about 72 cookies.

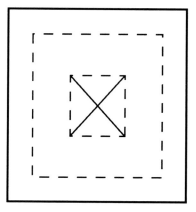

Buckle
Clip in center

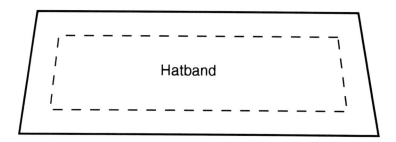

Hatband

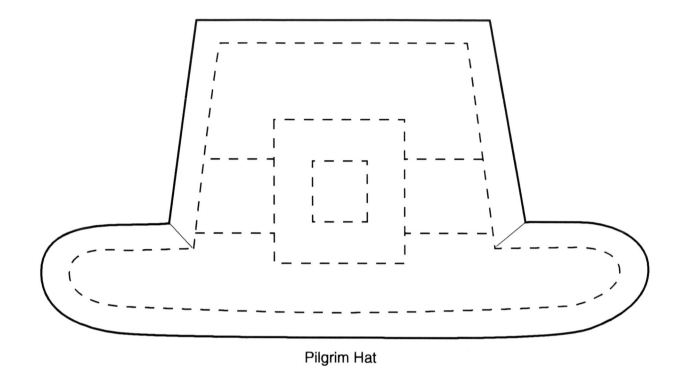

Pilgrim Hat

HAPPY THANKSGIVING

Bow Baking Pan Cover
and Wall Hanging

When you need to play Santa Claus, wrap up a pan of Fruit and Nut Brownies with this splendid patchwork bow. The red dot and candy stripe fabrics are fun to piece and make the bow and streamers appear to twist and turn. Once the brownies are eaten (these dried fruit and nut treats will go fast!), the cover converts to a wall hanging for the kitchen, den, or any corner that could use a boost of Christmas cheer. The cover is 9¼" × 9¼", to fit a 9" x 9" baking pan.

SUPPLIES

⅜ yard dark green print fabric
scraps of white, red/white candy stripe, and
    red/white dotted fabrics
1⅛ yards red piping
¾ yard ¾" green ribbon
1 skein each red and green embroidery floss
fiberfill batting
2 ½" plastic crochet rings
4 ½" snaps

CUTTING GUIDE

1 white A (do not cut until embroidery is
    completed; see directions)
18 white B's
12 red/white candy stripe B's
6 red/white dotted B's
6 white C's
7 red/white candy stripe C's
4 red/white dotted C's
2 white D's
2 dark green print E strips 1½" × 7½"
2 dark green F strips 1½" × 9½"
1 dark green print back 9½" × 9½"
1 fiberfill batting square 9½" × 9½"

DIRECTIONS

Trace the block A outline, words, and dots on right side of white fabric. Place the fabric in an embroidery hoop. Using two strands floss in needle, embroider words in green backstitch and dots in red satin stitch. Cut out A on marked lines.

Sew 12 striped B's and 12 white B's together in pairs for 12 B/B stripe squares. Sew 6 dotted B's and 6 white B's together in pairs for 6 B/B dotted squares. Referring to row diagrams and color key, join pieced B's and C's together to make rows 1, 2, 3, and 5; take care to position diagonal seams as shown in individual row diagrams. Join pieced B's with C and 2 D's to make row 4. Sew two remaining pieced B's to C's, then join to sides of embroidered A to make rows 6 and 7. Join rows to complete the bow patchwork. Frame the block by sewing two dark green print E strips to the top and bottom edges, then two dark green print F strips to the side edges. Block should measure 9½" × 9½".

Place fiberfill square under patchwork block and baste with long, loose stitches. Quilt all white A, B, C, and D blocks in outline quilting. Sew red piping around the edge of patchwork block, butting ends for a neat finish (page 20). Place patchwork

and back together, right sides facing and edges matching. Stitch all around, securing fiberfill and piping in seam; leave an opening along one straight edge for turning. Trim batting close to stitching, then turn right side out. Sew closed from back, making tiny stitches.

Sew crochet rings to top back corners of cover for hanging loops. Cut ribbon in two, for one 13" and one 14" piece. Fold ends 1/4" to wrong side and stitch down for a neat finish. Separate snaps into male and female halves. Sew male snap halves to ends of ribbon on wrong side. Sew female snaps to midpoint of each edge on patchwork back. Cover brownies with plastic wrap, then set bow patchwork cover on top. Snap ribbons in place to secure; longer ribbon will fit over handles at sides of dish.

Fruit and Nut Brownies

1 20.5-oz. package brownie mix
½ cup dried apricots
½ cup dried apples
½ cup dried, pitted prunes
½ cup raisins
½ cup walnuts, chopped
½ cup pecans, chopped

9" square baking pan, greased
4½" × 2½" × 1½" individual loaf pan, greased

Preheat oven to temperature specified on mix package. Chop apricots, apples, and prunes into small pieces. Prepare mix as directed on box. Stir in chopped dried fruits and nuts. Spoon and spread mixture into a greased 9" baking pan until batter reaches halfway up pan sides. Spoon remaining batter in an individual greased loaf pan. Bake as directed on mix package. Let cool in pans for several hours. Cut cake into 3-inch squares. Cut loaf into 4 slices.
Makes 13 brownies.

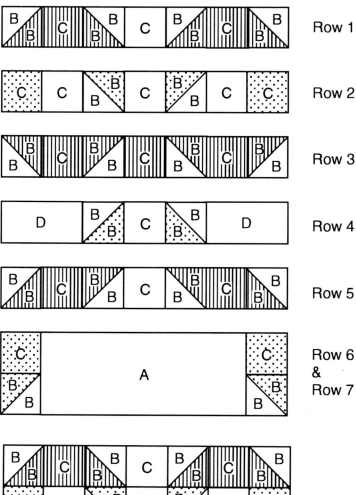

Row 1

Row 2

Row 3

Row 4

Row 5

Row 6
&
Row 7

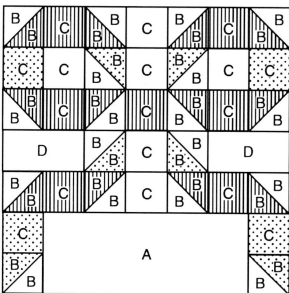

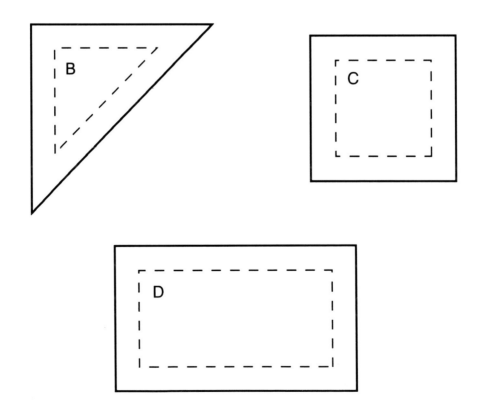

Evergreen Tote

Four evergreen trees and lively red patchwork convey the Christmas spirit wherever this tote is carried. For gift-giving, the tote is filled with easy-to-bake Christmas Cranberry Bread. The lucky recipient will find the tote handy later on for transporting small holiday gifts, party favors, decorations, or other items of the season. Tote is a roomy 17½" × 17½".

SUPPLIES

1⅛ yard dark red/white print fabric
⅛ yard red/white striped fabric
⅛ yard red pindot fabric
⅛ yard dark green print fabric
⅛ yard white fabric
scraps of dark olive print and brown print fabrics
2 yards ¼" dark green braid
fiberfill batting

CUTTING GUIDE

10 red/white striped A's
10 red pindot A's
 4 dark green print B's
 8 white C's
 4 dark olive print D's
 4 brown print D's
 8 white E's
 2 dark red/white print F strips 2½" × 14½"
 2 dark red/white print G strips 2½" × 18½"
 2 dark red/white print H's
 1 dark red/white print back 18½" × 18½"
 2 dark red/white print linings 18½" × 18½"
 2 fiberfill batting squares 18½" × 18½"
 2 fiberfill batting strips 1½" × 15"

DIRECTIONS

Assemble patchwork blocks and strips following Diagram 1. Sew red/white striped A's and red pindot A's together in pairs for 10 A/A rectangles (a). Sew A/A rectangles together in pairs for 5 pieced A squares (b). Sew 2 white C's to each B for 4 tree blocks (c). Sew 2 white E's to sides of each brown D for four D/E strips (d). Sew 4 dark olive print D's to ends of 2 D/E strips (e).

Assemble patchwork blocks into rows following Diagram 2. Sew 2 pieced A blocks to white edges of tree block for rows 1 and 3; make sure striped A's touch base of tree at corners. Sew point edge of 2 tree blocks to sides of a pieced A block for row 2.

Assemble the tote front following Diagram 3. Join rows 1, 2, and 3 together. Sew 2 shorter D/E strips to top and bottom of large pieced block, then sew 2 longer D/E strips to sides. Frame the block by sewing 2 dark red/white print F's to the top and bottom edges, then 2 dark red/white print G's to the side edges. Finished tote front should measure 18½" × 18½".

Lay tote front on top of a batting square, right side up, and baste with long, loose stitches. Quilt all the white C's and E's in outline quilting. Remove all basting threads. Place tote front and back together, right sides facing and edges matching. Place remaining batting square on tote back, and pin all around. Carefully stitch side and bottom edges together, catching batting in seam; leave top edge open. Trim batting close to stitching, clip corners, and turn right side out. Topstitch ¼" from raw edge all around. Sew linings together in same

manner as tote; do not turn. Press top edge of lining ¼" to wrong side.

Make handles following Diagram 4. Press one long edge of each H strip ¼" to wrong side (a). Lay on a flat surface, wrong side up, and center batting strip on top. Fold each H strip around batting strip, overlapping raw edge ¼" at center; pin in place (b). Topstitch along folded edge through all layers, securing fabric to batting. Hand-sew braid to center of each handle, concealing topstitching. Pin handles, right sides facing and raw edges matching, to top edge of tote front and back 5½" in from side seams. Stitch ¼" from edges over previous stitching. Press tote top edge to wrong side along stitching line, so handles pop up.

Insert the lining into the bag between the front and back batting, matching seams and folds. Pin folded edges together, then machine-stitch all around through all layers, catching in handles as you go. Hand-sew braid around top edge, concealing machine stitching.

Christmas Cranberry Bread

4 tablespoons margarine
2 cups granulated sugar
2 large eggs, beaten
½ cup orange juice
1 cup water
1 teaspoon vanilla extract
4 cups sifted all-purpose flour
3 teaspoons baking powder
1 teaspoon salt
1 cup walnuts, finely chopped
2 cups cranberries, halved or coarsely chopped in blender

two 9" × 5" × 3" loaf pans, greased

Preheat oven to 325°F. In a large mixing bowl, cream margarine and sugar together until smooth. Mix in the eggs, orange juice, water, and vanilla extract until well blended. In a medium bowl, sift together flour, baking powder, and salt and add gradually to margarine mixture while mixing on low speed. Fold in nuts and cranberries. Pour batter into greased loaf pans, scraping excess from sides of bowl with a rubber spatula, and spread evenly to sides of pans. Bake 1 hour, or until testing straw comes out clean. Cool in pans.
Makes 18 1-inch-thick slices.

Diagram 1
Blocks and Strips

Diagram 2
Row Assembly

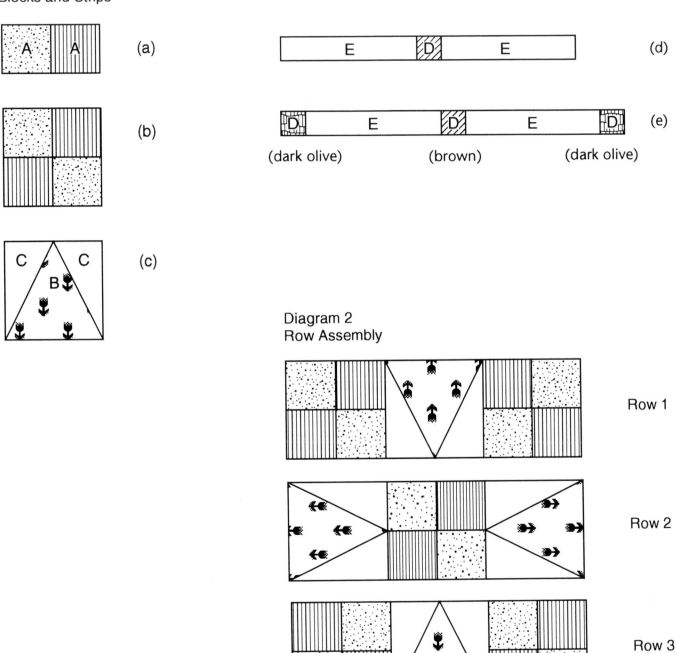

Diagram 3
Tote Front Assembly

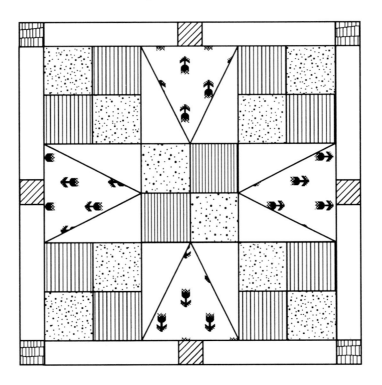

Diagram 4

(a)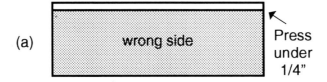

Press
under
1/4"

(b)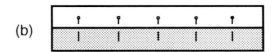

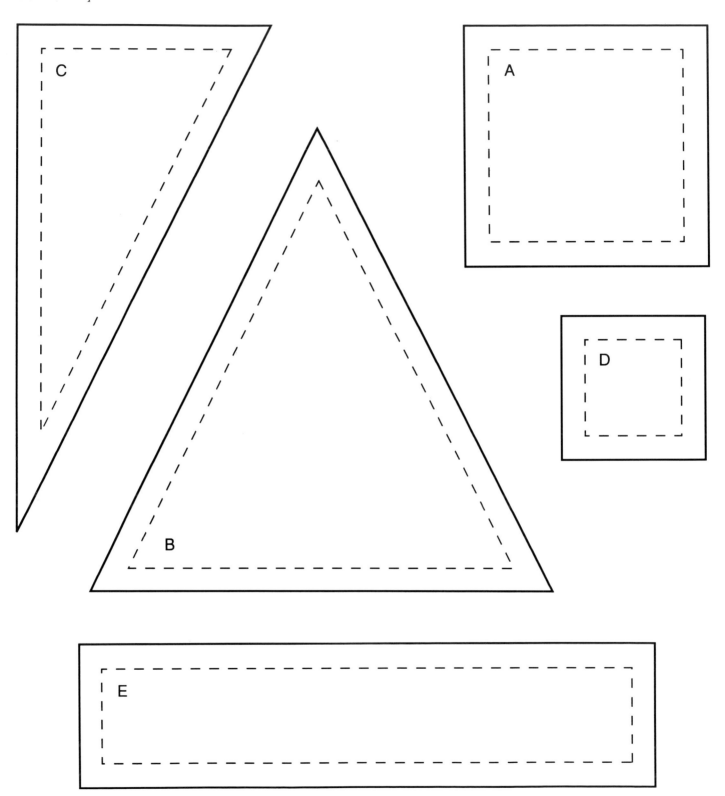

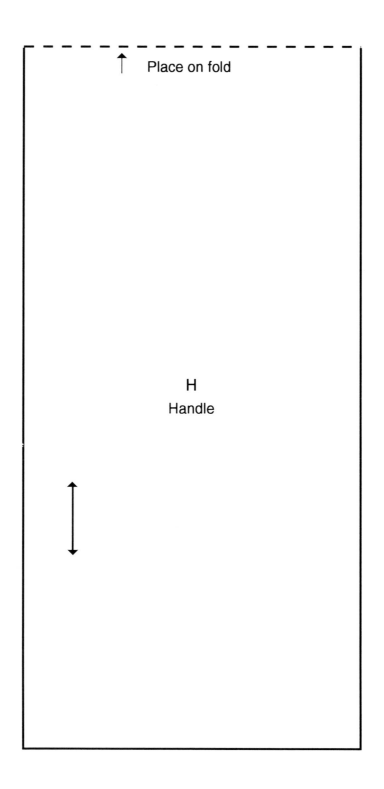

Place on fold

H
Handle

Grapevine Wreath Plate

To transform a purchased grapevine wreath into a gift container, I simply glued a plastic plate to the bottom. A ring of patchwork hearts, ribbon, and berries glued around the top edge sets the Christ-. mas theme. I nestled thick chunks of my husband's African Peanut Brittle inside. John lived in Africa for three years as a young boy, and he remembers vividly the foods of his childhood, which included exotic peanut soups, salads, and desserts. Peanut brittle remains one of his favorites. The wreath is about 12" across.

SUPPLIES

12" grapevine wreath
9" red plastic plate
scraps of red plaid and green print fabrics
 2 yards 1¼" dark green ribbon
scraps of fiberfill
artificial berries
glue gun

CUTTING GUIDE

4 patchwork heart fronts (assembled from 8 red plaid and 8 green print 3" × 3" squares; see directions)
4 green print hearts

DIRECTIONS

Make 4 patchwork hearts following Patchwork Block Diagram. Sew red plaid squares and green print squares together in pairs to make 8 rectangles (a). Sew rectangles together in pairs to make 4 pieced red/green blocks (b). Mark heart pattern on right side of each block, matching straight solid lines on pattern to seams on blocks. Cut out hearts on marked lines.

Sew patchwork hearts and green print hearts together, right sides facing and edges matching; leave opening for turning. Clip curves, bottom point, and top center. Turn right side out. Stuff each heart lightly with fiberfill. Sew opening closed with tiny stitches. Quilt inside each patchwork piece in outline quilting.

Center the grapevine wreath on top of the plate and glue in place. Cut ribbon in half, for two 36" lengths. Tie one end of each ribbon into a bow about 4" across, so a single long streamer extends on the left side. Glue bows to top and bottom of wreath. Referring to Wreath Diagram, wind streamers in and out of topmost vines, gluing end under bow on opposite side. Glue quilted hearts to top, bottom, and sides of wreath. Glue berries to wreath and hearts to fill out bare spaces.

African Peanut Brittle

2 cups granulated sugar
1 cup brown sugar
1½ cups light corn syrup
1 cup water
2 cups unroasted Spanish peanuts, shelled
2 tablespoons butter
½ teaspoon salt
2 teaspoons vanilla extract
1 tablespoon baking soda

baking sheets with rim, well buttered

Combine sugars, corn syrup, and water in a heavy saucepan and bring to boil, stirring constantly until candy thermometer reaches 240°F. Stir in peanuts, continuing to boil until thermometer reaches 300°F. Remove from heat. Add butter, salt, vanilla extract, and baking soda, and stir quickly just to combine ingredients (baking soda will cause mixture to foam). Pour mixture onto well buttered baking sheets and quickly spread it out to edges with a wooden spoon to a ¼- to ⅜-inch thickness. Let cool completely. Break into pieces, being careful not to cut your fingers on the sharp candy edges.
Makes 3 pounds of candy.

Patchwork
Block
Diagram

(a)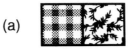

(b)

Wreath
Diagram

X = heart placement

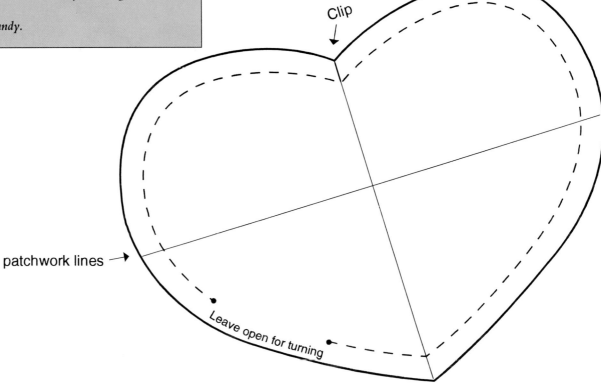

Holiday Holly Basket

Quilted holly leaves with berries (my favorite Christmas motif) run around the edge of a gift basket that has been painted white. When you are asked to bring dessert to a holiday gathering, pack up a basket like this with generous wedges of Celebration Poppy Seed Cake wrapped individually in plastic wrap. I always include a small jar of raspberry glaze to drizzle over the cake just before it is served. Basket is 10" across × 7" high, excluding handle.

SUPPLIES

basket 10" across × 7" high, excluding handle
white nontoxic spray paint
⅜ yard dark green fabric
⅛ yard red/white plaid fabric
scrap of red pindot fabric
scrap of fiberfill
fabric stiffener
glue gun

CUTTING GUIDE

28 dark green holly leaves
17 red pindot holly berries
 1 red/white plaid strip 2" × 44" (trim off selvages)

DIRECTIONS

Spray the basket with white paint, following paint manufacturer's directions. Let dry, then spray a second coat. Let dry completely.

Cut the red/white plaid strip into one 18" strip for bow loops and two 13" strips for streamers. Following manufacturer's directions, saturate strips with fabric stiffener. As each strip begins to dry, shape it, referring to the Bow Diagram. First, bring the ends of the longer strip together to form a circle. Pinch the circle edges together at the center to form two loops, each about 3½" long (a). Cut a V-shaped notch in one end of the two remaining strips (b). Shape each strip into a wavy S-shape for bow streamer (c). When bow pieces are stiff, glue loops to streamers (d). Set bow aside to dry thoroughly.

Place 28 dark green holly leaves together in pairs, right sides facing and edges matching. Sew together, leaving one straight edge open for turning. Clip curves and points, being careful not to snip into stitching. Turn right side out. Stuff lightly with fiberfill. Sew opening closed with tiny stitches. Quilt down center of each leaf. You should have 14 holly leaves.

To make berries, hand-sew a running stitch ⅛" from edge of each cutout berry. Draw up thread as tightly as possible to form berry; knot thread ends securely. You should have 17 berries.

Glue 12 holly leaves to outside rim of basket. Glue 15 berries in random clusters to ends of leaves. Glue stiffened bow to top of basket handle, so streamers cascade down to basket rim. Glue remaining leaves and berries to top of bow. After basket is packed with cake and glaze, lay a few sheets of red or green tissue paper on top.

Celebration Poppy Seed Cake

2¾ cups granulated sugar
1 cup vegetable oil
3 large eggs
1½ teaspoons vanilla extract
1 teaspoon almond extract
3 cups sifted all-purpose flour
2 tablespoons poppy seeds
1½ teaspoons baking powder
½ teaspoon salt
1½ cups milk

9" × 5" × 3" loaf pan, greased and floured

Preheat oven to 350°F. In a large mixing bowl, mix sugar, oil, eggs, vanilla extract, and almond extract until well blended and smooth. In a separate large bowl, sift together flour, poppy seeds, baking powder, and salt. Add sifted dry ingredients and milk alternately to sugar mixture, beginning and ending with dry ingredients, and mix well after each addition. Pour batter into greased and floured pan and spread it evenly to the sides. Bake about 50 minutes, or until testing straw comes out clean. Let cool in pan. To serve, slice into individual servings and drizzle with raspberry glaze.
Makes 9 1-inch-thick slices.

Raspberry Glaze

1 cup confectioners' sugar
¼ cup raspberry juice
¼ teaspoon almond extract

Whisk ingredients together in a small bowl until well blended and sugar is dissolved.
Makes ⅔ cup.

Bow Diagram

Center

(a)

3 1/2" 3 1/2"

(b)

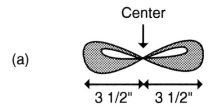

(c)

(d)

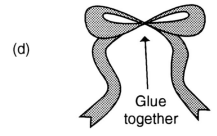

Glue together

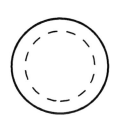

Holly Berry

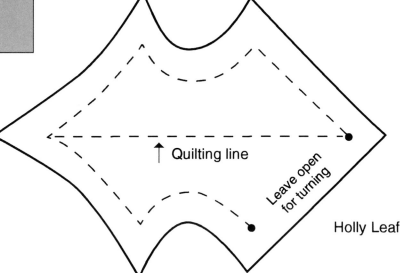

↑ Quilting line

Leave open for turning

Holly Leaf

Mistletoe Wreath
Gift Bag and Tag

The holiday wreath that adorns this gift bag can be removed and used as a decoration for many Christmases to come. The miniature wreath is decorated with fabric mistletoe berries and leaves. Gold ribbon and foil-wrapped chocolate kisses add holiday sparkle. The wreath and gift tag both hint at the treat inside: Peanut Butter Chocolate Kiss Cookies. Chewy and peanut-buttery, they make a welcome family gift. Bag is 10½" × 8"; tag is 2" × 3½".

GIFT BAG SUPPLIES

8" × 10½" purchased red gift bag
6" bleached or natural grapevine wreath
⅛ yard green pindot fabric
⅛ yard white fabric
1⅛ yard ½" gold metallic ribbon
4 Hershey's almond and chocolate kisses in gold foil wrap
5 sprigs baby's breath
glue gun

GIFT BAG CUTTING GUIDE

28 green pindot mistletoe leaves
12 white mistletoe berries

GIFT BAG DIRECTIONS

Sew 28 green pindot mistletoe leaves together in pairs, leaving short straight edges open for turning. Clip curves, and turn right side out. Fold raw edges ¼" to inside and sew closed with tiny stitches. You should have 14 leaves.

To make berries, hand-sew a running stitch ⅛" from edge of each cutout berry. Draw up thread as tightly as possible to form berry; knot thread ends securely. You should have 12 berries.

Attach ribbon to wreath following Diagram 1. Cut four 6" lengths of gold metallic ribbon. Bend each piece into a loop and glue the ends together (a). Cut the remaining ribbon in half for two streamers each approximately 8" long. Glue the streamers to the center top of wreath so ends cascade down sides; glue ribbon to wreath as necessary to hold shape. Glue four loops to top of wreath, so glued edges meet in center (b).

Decorate wreath following Diagram 2. Put a dot of glue on end of each mistletoe leaf, then pinch edges together to give leaf dimension. Glue leaves in position around wreath. Glue berries to leaves and wreath rounded side up, to conceal stitching. Glue four gold foil–wrapped Kisses to top, bottom, and sides of wreath. Insert sprigs of baby's breath into wreath to fill in bare spaces. Apply glue generously to back of wreath at top and bottom and affix to front of gift bag.

CHRISTMAS HUGS AND KISSES

TAG SUPPLIES

scrap of white fabric
⅓ yard ½" white lace
1 skein each red and green embroidery floss
½ yard ¹⁄₁₆" gold ribbon

TAG CUTTING GUIDE

2 white tags (do not cut until embroidery is
  completed; see directions)

TAG DIRECTIONS

Trace the tag outline twice on right side of white
fabric. Trace the words and heart inside one tag.
Place the fabric in an embroidery hoop (page 17).
Using two strands floss in needle, embroider the
words in green backstitch and the heart in red satin
stitch.

  Cut out both tags on the marked lines. Place
front and back tags together, right sides facing.
Stitch all around, leaving an opening at top for
turning. Turn right side out. Sew opening closed
with tiny stitches. Slip straight edge of lace just
under edge of tag; baste all around, folding short
ends to wrong side for a neat finish. Topstitch
along edge of tag all around. Tie an overhand knot
at midpoint of rose ribbon. Position knot on back
of tag at spot marked by × on pattern and sew in
place. Tie ribbon ends around gift bag handle.

Peanut Butter Chocolate Kiss Cookies

½ cup margarine, softened at room temperature
½ cup granulated sugar
½ cup light brown sugar
½ cup creamy peanut butter
1 large egg
1 teaspoon vanilla extract
1¼ cups sifted all-purpose flour
¾ teaspoon baking soda
approximately 24 Hershey's chocolate Kisses,
  unwrapped

cookie sheets, greased

Preheat oven to 350°F. In a medium mixing bowl,
cream together margarine and sugars until fluffy and
light yellow, then cream in peanut butter until creamy
and light brown. Add egg and vanilla extract and beat
well. Sift together flour and baking soda and add gradually to peanut butter mixture, mixing until well blended. Chill dough, covered, in refrigerator for ½ hour.
Form dough into 1½-inch balls and set 1½ inches apart
on a greased cookie sheet. Press flat side of a chocolate
Kiss into each dough ball, flattening the ball slightly.
Bake for 10 minutes, or until golden brown. Cool on
wire racks 20 minutes or longer before eating.
Makes about 24 cookies.

Diagram 1

(a)  ← Glue ends together here.

(b)

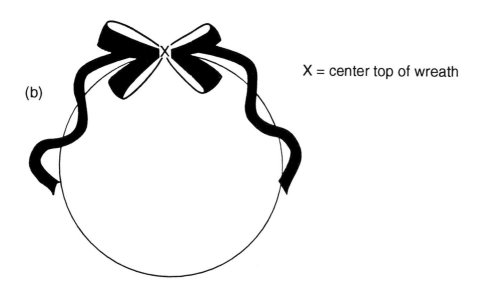

X = center top of wreath

Diagram 2
Mistletoe leaves, berry and chocolate Kiss placement

Note: Fill in with sprigs of
baby's breath to give the
wreath a full look

○   = Mistletoe berry

⬭   = Mistletoe leaf

△   = Chocolate Kiss (gold foil almond)

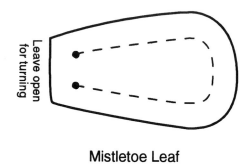

Leave open for turning

Mistletoe Leaf

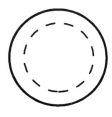

Berry

Leave open for turning

X

CHRISTMAS
HUGS AND
KISSES ♡

X = Ribbon placement

Index

All of us at Meredith® Press are dedicated to offering you, our customer, the best books we can create. We are particularly concerned that all of our instructions for making projects are clear and accurate. Please address your correspondence to Customer Service, Meredith Press, 150 East 52nd Street, New York, NY 10022.

If you would like to order additional copies of any of our books, call 1-800-678-2803 or check with your local bookstore.